# Hiking Waterfalls
# in Virginia

# Hiking Waterfalls in Virginia

### A Guide to the State's Best Waterfall Hikes

**Andy Thompson**

GUILFORD, CONNECTICUT
HELENA, MONTANA

An imprint of Rowman & Littlefield
Falcon, FalconGuides, and Outfit Your Mind are registered trademarks of Rowman & Littlefield.

Distributed by NATIONAL BOOK NETWORK

Copyright © 2015 by Rowman & Littlefield
Photos: Andy Thompson, except photo on page 183, licensed by Shutterstock.com
Maps: Melissa Baker © Rowman & Littlefield

British Library Cataloguing-in-Publication Information available
Library of Congress Cataloging-in-Publication Data available
ISBN 978-0-7627-9638-0 (paperback)
ISBN 978-1-4930-1445-3 (electronic)

♾™ The paper used in this publication meets the minimum requirements of American National Standard for Information Sciences—Permanence of Paper for Printed Library Materials, ANSI/NISO Z39.48-1992.

# Contents

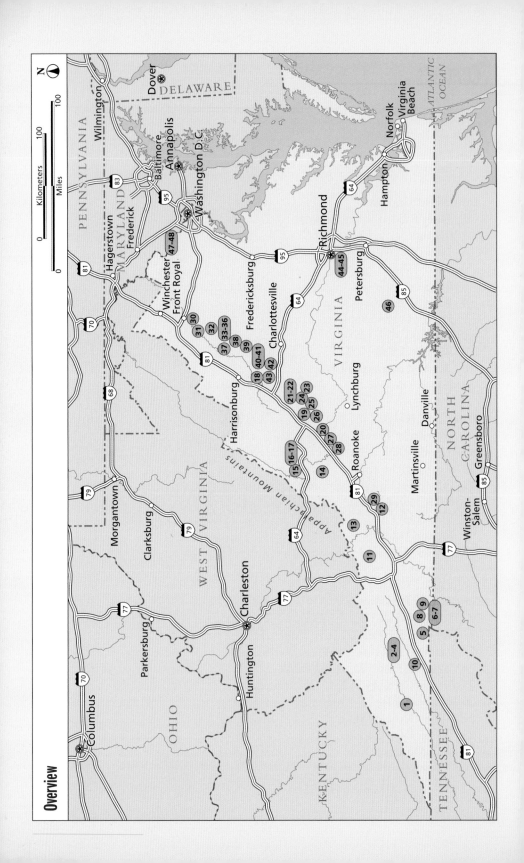

# Overview

## Shenandoah National Park

## Piedmont

## Northern Virginia

# Introduction

What is it about a waterfall? What pleasure receptors in the brain light up in the presence of a mountain stream cascading over a granite ledge into a deep pool? I may not be qualified to answer that question, but after spending the past year researching and writing this book, I know it is irrefutably true that waterfalls exert a powerful, mysterious hold on us.

Think of the last time you hiked to a waterfall near you. Maybe you started off at the trailhead where you couldn't even see the waterway that would eventually produce the falls. Maybe you heard it first as you hiked, then came up alongside it. As you kept walking in the shade of the forest, more side streams entered and the creek grew. Soon you could hear the falls in the distance. Do you remember the sense of anticipation at that instant? For me, that moment is almost as magical as reaching the falls itself: It's out there! You keep hiking, almost skipping down the trail, until you reach the falls. Maybe it comes with a view of the valley below. Maybe it's a classic woodland falls, with mosses growing on the rocks nearby. Maybe it's a sheer drop, with an undercut rock behind it that begs to be explored.

*Continue past Big Rock Falls in Shenandoah National Park and find President Herbert Hoover's trout fishing camp. History and scenery on one relatively easy hike (hike 5).*

*Comers Creek Falls is a lovely woodland cataract in southwest Virginia a short hike from the parking lot (hike 8).*

One of the great things about Virginia waterfalls is their variety. Many have commonalities, but no two are alike. Shenandoah National Park has the greatest concentration of falls in the state. Many are very close together, but there isn't a single one that you can skip because it's so much like another. That's true in Shenandoah and throughout the state. Falling Spring Falls is a travertine falls, but so is the Waterfall at Falls Ridge, and they look very different. The hikes to South River Falls and Lewis Falls both end with views of the falls and sweeping panoramas of the valleys below them. But the hikes have very little in common, despite being just a few miles apart. At times I'll compare one cascade to another, but each is unique, like a snowflake or fingerprint. And each will affect you in a different way.

This book is an invitation to explore. I hope through my own explorations and detailed note taking, I've taken the labor and stress out of finding and hiking to these falls. Just open up the book to a page, any page, and see if that falls catches your eye. Or check the Trail Finder feature to see hikes sorted by difficulty and those I consider my favorites. If you're limited to a certain geographical area, this book makes it easy to find waterfalls near you as well.

My number-one goal in writing this book was accuracy. There's nothing worse than getting lost, whether on the trail or on the way to the trail. But I also hope it entertains. Choosing waterfall hikes—as opposed to summit hikes or any other kind of hike—is a great way to see the mountainous parts of Virginia (and a few other places as well). It means there's always a payoff at the end, one both obvious and mysterious. So get out there and explore—and don't forget your camera!

*The hike to Overall Run Falls offers this lovely mountain view as well as a view of the falls (hike 31).*

# How to Use This Guide

Because Virginia's waterfalls are spread out across (almost) all of the state's physiographic regions, the first thing you'll notice when you page through the listings is that the waterfalls are separated by geography. Makes sense, right? If you're spending some time hiking around Abingdon, Virginia, you'll want to know which waterfalls are nearby. What good would an alphabetical listing be?

For each waterfall hike (some hikes feature multiple waterfalls), my goal is to give you absolutely all the information you'll need to find the trail, navigate it safely, reach the waterfall, and enjoy yourself along the way. You'll find a map of the trail and falls; a short introduction, to give you a taste of what you're about to experience; then the hike specs: essentials like the height of the falls, the length of the hike (round-trip), a difficulty rating, a trail surface description, and more.

You'll notice I also include the *DeLorme Virginia Atlas & Gazetteer* page number and coordinates for each hike. If you intend to become a Virginia waterfall hound, the second purchase you should make is that atlas (the first, of course, is the book you currently hold in your hands!). My DeLorme atlas is shredded, dog-eared, and written on, and it's my second copy. Don't leave home on a waterfall journey without one.

After the hike specs you'll see the "Finding the Trailhead" section. My intention here is to get you from the nearest major road (often, but not always, an interstate) to the trailhead. For many of the hikes, this is not a difficult task. Just follow directions and you're there. For others, you'll drive on gravel roads that can be rutted and generally rough going (especially after rains or in the winter). But take heart: The vast majority of even the fire roads and country roads in Virginia are marked well enough to get you where you need to go. I won't lead you astray. But if all else fails, I've also included the GPS coordinates for the trailhead in this section.

Next comes "The Hike," where I detail what to expect when the hiking boots are on, the backpack is laden with water, trail mix, and a camera, and you set off in search of that hard-to-describe experience that only waterfalls offer. Here you'll find history, geology, and flora and fauna to look for and any other tidbits that might make your journey more context-rich and enjoyable.

Finally, there's the "Miles and Directions" section, where I've detailed thorough hiking directions down to the tenth of a mile. "0.0 Miles—Look for the information kiosk at the parking lot, and follow yellow blazes onto Little Stony Trail. . . . 0.2 Cross Little Stony Creek just upstream of the top of upper falls. . . . 0.4 Continue on the trail to a bridge over middle falls, then alongside of it. . . ." You get the idea. If it's a roadside hike, there is no "Miles and Directions" section.

## A Word about Private Property

If I had included every waterfall on private property, there would probably be at least another fifty entries in this book (and I'd be in jail for trespassing!). But, of course,

I can't do that. There are a number of private property waterfalls included in this book, but if you follow my directions—which I recommend—you will view them from public locations. Some you can see from the roadside, some are places, like the Nature Conservancy preserves, that want you to come experience their waterfall. It's worth stressing, however, that private property boundaries are to be respected at all times.

## A Word about Definitions

What exactly is a waterfall? When you have to make decisions like I did for this book, that question enters your mind a lot. How high does a waterfall have to be to qualify? How wide? How much water needs to be flowing over it?

Many Virginia falls don't compare to Colorado falls, say, in height. There are likely more 12-footers in this book than the Colorado one. But what many lack in height, they more than make up for in other qualities. Big Rock Falls on Whitetop Laurel Creek near Damascus won't blow you away with its height, but it's along the Virginia Creeper Trail in the shadow of Mount Rogers and is surrounded by absolutely gorgeous hemlock forests and rock walls. It's worth the trip.

On the other hand, there were a number of falls that were on the cusp of being separate entries that didn't make the cut. I like to think I applied a consistent rationale for these decisions, but sometimes it came down to a gut feeling. "Would I make a separate trip for this single falls?" I'd ask myself. "Would I tell a friend to make this trip?" There may be a falls or two that you know of that didn't make this book. Chances are I knew about it, but it just didn't make the cut. Blame my gut.

I also made a rule early on that I would not recommend waterfalls that people have to bushwhack to. Virginia has its share of falls deep in the woods with no real trail to them, but rest assured, any waterfall in the state of Virginia that you have to bushwhack to probably isn't worth bushwhacking to. That's the thing about waterfalls—their power is so great, people seek them out. They always have. And when people seek something out over the course of generations, even centuries, there's (almost) always a record of those people. In the forest that record is a trail.

## Weather

The Blue Ridge and Appalachian Mountains in Virginia don't generally have wild weather swings like some ranges out west, but weather certainly isn't the same here as it is in Washington, DC, or Richmond or Virginia Beach. I once went to Grayson Highlands State Park, next to Mount Rogers, Virginia's tallest peak at 5,729 feet, in April. It was 70°F that day, but the park ranger told me that two days earlier the high was in the 30s and they received a couple of inches of snow.

Generally speaking, and not surprisingly, you'll find most of these waterfalls in Virginia's mountains, and Virginia's mountains are cooler than the countryside below. Since none of the hikes in this book are multiday hikes, it shouldn't be a big deal to throw in a warmer jacket or rain gear. You just never know how the day will change from when you set out from home to when you set out on the trail.

## Safety

Most of the safety points I'll make here will be obvious to the experienced hiker. But a little refresher never hurt.

*Share your plan.* Whether you're heading out into the national forest or looking for a roadside falls, tell someone about it. You never know what can happen out there.

*Gear up.* Hiking boots and layered clothes that are seasonally appropriate are key. So is a good backpack that spreads out the load. Always bring water, no matter how short the hike.

*Prepare for the worst.* If you want to make one of these hikes into a longer, multiday affair, carry the essentials, like a flashlight, first-aid kit, map, compass, fire starter, and extra clothing. It's worth having a little bit of extra weight in the pack if things go south and you have to change plans in a hurry.

*Bring a towel.* Who knows, the mood to swim might just strike you, and there are lots of good swimming holes associated with these waterfalls. And a few of these hikes call for fording creeks. It's better to take off one's boots and socks, dry off, and then put them back on, than to hike with cold, wet feet.

*Watch the ledge!* These are waterfalls we're talking about, after all, many with high, sheer drops. Some, like Crabtree Falls, have signs warning hikers about deaths that have occurred there in the past. Use good judgment and stay away from edges, especially if you're bringing dogs or children with you.

## Respecting Our Mother

That's Mother Nature, of course. These hikes will take you through some of the most beautiful places in the state, but from time to time, you'll see that not everyone who's come before you respects that beauty as much as they should. It's just not that hard: If you pack something in, pack it out. I made it my mission to pick up at least one piece of someone else's litter on every hike.

Similarly, depending on the time of year you hike, you'll pass gorgeous wildflowers, blooming rhododendrons, and incredible geologic formations. All you need is a camera to take them home with you.

# Trail Finder

To get our readers started on the hikes that best suit their interests and abilities, we include this simple trail finder that categorizes each of the hikes in the book into a helpful list. Your hikes can fall under more than one category.

### Roadside

### Easy

### Easy/Moderate

### Moderate

### Moderate/Strenuous

### Strenuous

### Author's Favorites

# Map Legend

## Municipal

≡(81)≡ Interstate Highway

≡(178)≡ US Highway

≡(640)≡ State Road

≡(721)≡ Local/County Road

= = = = Gravel Road

= = = = Unpaved Road

⊢—⊢—⊢ Railroad

– - – - – State Boundary

## Trails

------ Featured Trail

- - - - - Trail

## Water Features

⬭ Body of Water

〜 River/Creek

〜/〜 Intermittent Stream

≋ Waterfall

o⌐ Spring

## Symbols

〕〔 Bridge

■ Building/Point of Interest

⛺ Campground

🅿 Parking

〕〔 Pass

▲ Peak/Elevation

🔤 Picnic Area

🏞 Scenic View

o Town

⑳ Trailhead

❓ Visitor/Information Center

## Land Management

▢ National Park/Forest

▢ State/County Park

# Southwest Virginia

This region of the state is rugged and gorgeous and often alien to the average Virginian. Many people from the DC suburbs or the Norfolk area, if they've been out to southwest Virginia at all, have done so on the way through on I-81. Maybe that's due to the quirky nature of Virginia's geography. Most of southwest Virginia is simply a long drive from the state's population centers. The three falls on the Little Stony River, one of the most stunning natural places I've ever been, are closer to six other state capitals—Raleigh, North Carolina; Nashville, Tennessee; Charleston, West Virginia; Columbus, Ohio; Frankfort, Kentucky; and Columbia, South Carolina—than they are to Richmond. That's pretty amazing.

But for waterfall lovers, southwest Virginia is a must-see part of the state. You simply cannot miss the spectacular setting of the falls on the Little Stony or the stair-step beauty of the Falls of Dismal or the mountain scenery of falls in the Mount Rogers area. Not only are the cataracts in this region worth the drives to reach them, but the region itself beautiful, full of empty country roads, tiny towns, and much elevation change.

Keep in mind that a number of the waterfalls I include in this region are, geologically speaking, in the Valley and Ridge. I divided these up more by proximity than by geology. Could the Falls of Dismal go in the Valley and Ridge section? Sure, but it's closer to most of these falls than the falls in the Valley and Ridge. This division should make for more efficient waterfall hunting.

# 1 Three Falls on the Little Stony

Three falls that are all very different—and all gorgeous in their own right—await on this easy, 1-mile round-trip hike. The Falls of the Little Stony are three of my favorites and an absolute must-see Virginia waterfall destination.

**Height:** Upper falls: 25-foot vertical drop; middle falls: 10–15-foot cascade; lower falls: 35-foot cascade

**Start:** The Little Stony National Recreation Trail begins at the obvious trailhead in the gravel lot.

**Distance:** 1.0 mile out and back

**Difficulty:** Easy

**Canine compatibility:** Dogs allowed off-leash in the Jefferson National Forest

**Trail surface:** Wide and sometimes a bit rocky and rooty. Not steep.

**Hiking time:** About 30 minutes

**Blaze color:** Yellow

**County:** Scott

**Land status:** National Forest

**Trail contact:** Jefferson National Forest, (888) 265-0019; www.fs.usda.gov/gwj; Forest Supervisor's Office, 5162 Valleypointe Parkway, Roanoke 24019

**Maps:** *DeLorme, Virginia Atlas and Gazetteer:* page 20, A4

**Finding the trailhead:** From the town of Dungannon, head north on SR 72. Turn left onto CR 664, heading west, and drive just over 1 mile. Turn left onto FR 700, a gravel road. Drive 1.25 miles and turn left again onto FR 701, another gravel/dirt road. Continue just under a mile to the parking area on the left. This area is well marked. You'll feel like you're in the middle of nowhere, but it would be very hard to get lost here. **GPS:** N36 52.179' / W82 27.813'

*A trailside observation area offers a lovely elevated view of the lower falls on the Little Stony.*

# The Hike

Where should I begin with the three waterfalls on the Little Stony? This gem of a hike has something for almost everyone. The only people who won't fall in love with these falls are those who might have wanted a grueling workout. For everyone else the Little Stony has it all: three falls, all gorgeous and all different, all within a half mile of one another on a trail any able-bodied waterfall hound could hike in his or her sleep.

There are swimming holes, geologic wonders, thick rhododendrons, and towering eastern hemlocks. Simply put, this is a must-see for Virginia waterfall lovers.

The top falls might be the most impressive. After just 300 yards of hiking gently downhill, you'll cross a bridge just upstream of the lip of the falls. Keep going until you see the 20-yard spur trail down to the base of the beauty. There you'll find that Little Stony Creek pours over an overhanging ledge into a deep, green pool. With the

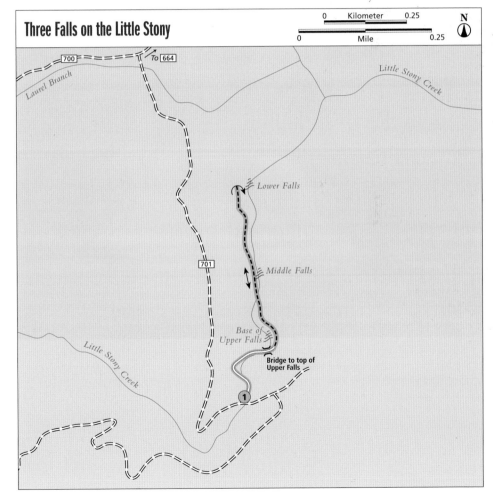

cave behind the splashdown zone easily accessible, you'll feel like you're on a movie set here.

A few hundred yards down the trail, you'll find the middle falls. It's not as high as its bookend sisters, but it's a worthy 10-to-15-foot waterfall in its own right. There's a small trail that allows hikers to scramble right to its base.

Four-tenths of a mile into your hike, the trail gets slightly steeper and more rooty. That means you're nearing the highest of the Little Stony's falls—the lower falls. This one is your classic stair-step cascade of about 25 feet, maybe 30. The trail is up above the top of the falls here, but a short scramble will bring you to the base easily enough, and another swimming area awaits if the weather permits. But remember, this is mountain water. It's cold all year round!

*The middle falls of the Little Stony may be the least impressive of the three but that doesn't mean it's unimpressive. This waterfall would stand out quite nicely if it wasn't sandwiched between two even more gorgeous falls.*

*The upper falls on the Little Stony might be my favorite waterfall in Virginia. Need I say more?*

## Miles and Directions

**0.0**  Look for the information kiosk at the parking lot, and follow yellow blazes onto the Little Stony National Recreation Trail.

**0.2**  Cross Little Stony Creek just upstream of the top of the upper falls (GPS: N36 52.268' / W82 27.707').

**0.4**  Continue on the trail to the bridge over the middle falls, then alongside the top of the waterfall itself. (GPS: N36 52.364' / W82 27.754').

**0.5**  Arrive at the observation area for the lower falls, then retrace your steps to the trailhead. (***Option:*** Scamper down to the base of the falls.) (GPS: N36 52.506' / W82 27.781')

**1.0**  Arrive back at the trailhead.

# 2 Big Falls

This is an easy, beautiful hike in a state-owned Natural Area Preserve protected for its singular geologic formation and many rare plant species.

**Height:** About 10 feet
**Start:** If you can't cross the river in your car, park in the upper lot and start your hike at the trailhead at the base of the suspension bridge.
**Distance:** 2.8 miles out and back if parking in upper lot
**Difficulty:** Easy/moderate
**Canine compatibility:** Dogs must be on a 6-foot leash in all Natural Area Preserves.
**Trail surface:** Wide gravel path
**Hiking time:** About 1 hour
**Blaze color:** None

**County:** Russell
**Land status:** Virginia Natural Area Preserve
**Trail contact:** Pinnacle NAP, dcr.virginia.gov/natural_heritage/natural_area_preserves/pinnacle.shtml; Department of Conservation and Recreation, Division of Natural Heritage, 217 Governor Street, Richmond 23219. Claiborne Woodall, Southwest Region Steward, (276) 676-5673
**Maps:** *DeLorme, Virginia Atlas and Gazetteer:* page 21, A7

**Finding the trailhead:** From Business US 19 in Lebanon, drive north on SR 82. After just over a mile, turn right on CR 640 and go just over 4 miles before turning left on CR 721. Follow this hard-packed gravel road to the parking area of Pinnacle Natural Area Preserve. If the water is low, you can follow the road right at Big Cedar Creek, then across the creek down to the lower lot. **GPS:** N36 38.644' / W81 44.401'

## The Hike

Pinnacle is one of just a few of Virginia's Natural Area Preserves that offer facilities for visitors. Some are off-limits entirely because they protect rare and delicate natural communities. At others you have to schedule a visit with the Department of Conservation and Recreation employee who's in charge of that NAP.

Luckily, Pinnacle is open to the public, and it operates a lot like a state park: It's got parking lots, trash cans, trail signage, and a picnic table or two. When I went in the middle of winter, Big Cedar Creek was swollen after a recent rain. Fording the creek and driving down to the lower lot was out of the question. So I parked at the first lot I came to and started hiking.

It wasn't bad having the extra distance, because the gravel road—aka Big Cedar Creek Trail—is flat and runs right along the river. And it was fun to bounce on the suspension bridge right there by the upper trailhead. Eventually you reach the lower lot, and from there you can easily follow the signs for the remaining 0.3 mile to get to the falls.

Big Falls won't blow you away with its drop, but it sits at a beautiful stretch of the river. Here the Big Cedar widens and makes a hard right a few hundred yards before entering the Clinch River. Just below the falls there's an island that you could probably rock-hop to in low water.

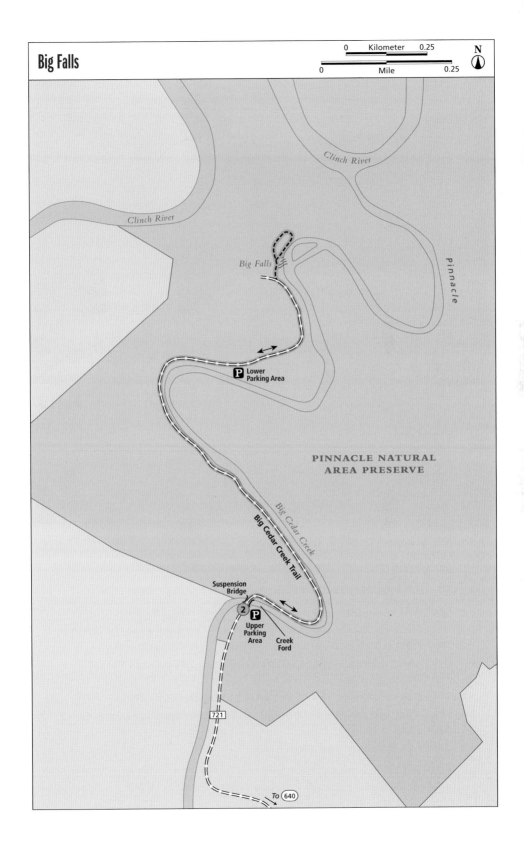

Big Falls

0    Kilometer    0.25

0    Mile    0.25

N

Clinch River

Clinch River

Clinch River

pinnacle

Big Falls

Lower Parking Area

PINNACLE NATURAL AREA PRESERVE

Big Cedar Creek

Big Cedar Creek Trail

Suspension Bridge

2

Upper Parking Area

Creek Ford

721

To 640

*Big Falls is located in one of the few state-owned Natural Area Preserves open to the public.*

## Miles and Directions

**0.0** Start at the upper parking area due to high flow on the Big Cedar. There's a trail map there, before you cross the suspension bridge. (*Option:* If the river level permits, park at and leave from the lower parking area for a 0.6-mile, 20-minute hike to the falls.)

**0.1** After crossing the suspension bridge, turn right and follow the Big Cedar Creek Trail downstream.

**1.0** Arrive at the lower parking area. Follow signs and stay on Big Cedar Creek Trail.

**1.4** Arrive at Big Falls (GPS: N36 38.057' / W81 44.941'), then retrace your steps to the parking area.

**2.8** Arrive back at the upper parking area.

# PINNACLE NATURAL AREA PRESERVE

If you hike to Big Falls in Russell County, you may wonder why the place you're hiking through, a state-owned Natural Area Preserve, is called "Pinnacle." Well, once you make it to Big Falls, keep on going along Big Cedar Creek and you'll see why.

The Pinnacle is a sheer spire of dolomite (a kind of limestone) that towers 400 feet above the Big Cedar and Clinch Rivers below. According to the state Department of Conservation and Recreation:

> The Pinnacle was created by the dissolving action of groundwater in combination with down-cutting of the gorge by Big Cedar Creek. Big Falls is formed where the creek passes over several layers of erosion-resistant sandstone.
>
> The geological diversity here has led to extraordinary biological diversity and created conditions suitable for several rare species. Growing in cracks and ledges along steep limestone cliffs are two globally rare plant species, Canby's mountain-lover (*Paxistima canbyi*) and Carolina saxifrage (*Saxifraga caroliniana*), and one state rarity, American harebell (*Campanula rotundifolia*).
>
> Another rare plant species, glade spurge (*Euphorbia purpurea*) is found along creek banks within the preserve. The Big Cedar Creek millipede (*Brachoria falcifera*) is known to exist only here and in a few other sites nearby.

The hike to Big Falls is relatively flat and not overly taxing. Why not throw in a little extra distance to find the geological oddity that gave the park its name?

# 3 Tank Hollow Falls

Tank Hollow Falls will surprise you with its height and location, tucked away at the edge of the town of Cleveland in far southwestern Virginia.

**Height:** 40 feet
**Start:** You won't need to leave your car to see this one, at least not in winter.
**Distance:** Roadside
**Difficulty:** Easy
**Canine compatibility:** N/A
**Trail surface:** N/A
**Hiking time:** 5-10 minutes

**Blaze color:** None
**County:** Russell
**Land status:** On private property, but viewed from public land
**Trail contact:** N/A
**Maps:** *DeLorme, Virginia Atlas and Gazetteer:* page 21, A6

**Finding the trailhead:** Start in Cleveland on SR 82. Head west onto CR 1204 at the Cleveland United Methodist Church. Go steeply uphill until you reach Cleveland Baptist Church. There at the front of Cleveland Baptist, you'll see one road that goes uphill. Don't take that. Right next to it you'll see a gravel road that goes steeply downhill. If you have a car with low clearance, you might want to park at the church and start walking. If you choose to drive, the gravel road will take you to the base of the falls. **GPS:** N36 56.425' / W82 09.299'

*Tank Hollow Falls will surprise you with its height and power.*

## The Hike

This is one for true waterfall hounds. The town of Cleveland is not really close to anything, so you have to go out of your way to see it. The falls itself is a nearly sheer cascade of about 40 feet bisected by the boundary between the town and the state-owned Cleveland Barrens Natural Area Preserve, home to a series of dolomite barrens and a number of rare plant and insect species.

I went in the winter when there were no leaves on the trees. I would imagine the views of the waterfall are somewhat obscured when the trees have leafed out. But no matter the season, this falls will surprise you with its tucked-away location, height, and power (at least after a rain).

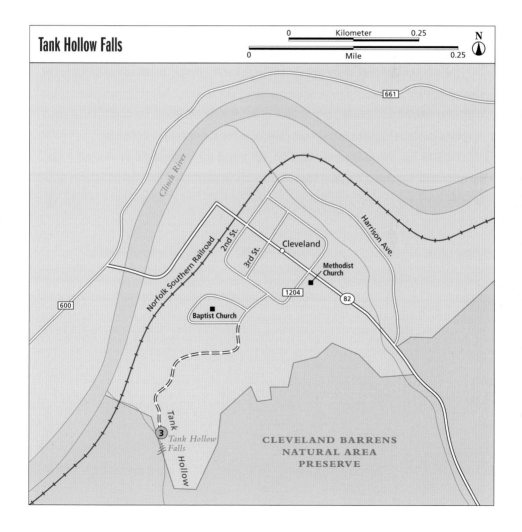

# CLEVELAND BARRENS

As you stand on the gravel road and look at Tank Hollow Falls in Cleveland, Virginia, note that the right side of the falls has a different owner than the left. On the right is the Cleveland Barrens Natural Area Preserve, state-owned land managed by the Department of Conservation and Recreation's Division of Natural Heritage.

Like the nearby Pinnacle Natural Area Preserve, Cleveland Barrens is home to a number of state and globally rare plant and insect species. According to the DCR's Natural Heritage Division, those species make this area home because of a geological formation called dolomite barrens. Dolomite bedrock contributes high levels of calcium and magnesium to the soil. At the NAP six significant barrens occur on steep, southwest-facing slopes. One of these, at 7 acres, is the largest such barren in Virginia. These unusual openings in the surrounding forest canopy are characterized by thin rocky soils and dominated by native, warm-season grasses.

The southwest aspect of the barrens produces harsh growing conditions as evidenced by stunted, drought-stressed red cedar scattered among the grasses. Most of the rare plants in the NAP occur within the dolomite barrens. Open, sunny habitat conditions are required to support the shade-intolerant species that are more typical of the midwestern United States.

The NAP has no public-access facilities, but a visit can be arranged by contacting Claiborne Woodall, Southwest Regional Supervisor for the DCR's Natural Heritage Division, at (276) 676-5673.

# 4 Three Falls on Tumbling Creek

In less than a mile along this rutted gravel road, you get three attractive falls. One, Twin Hollow Falls, is actually two creeks coming together and falling into Tumbling Creek.

**Height:** A sheer drop of 12 feet for Big Falls; 10 total feet of multiple drops onto ledges for the upper falls; 2 creeks each falling 40 feet into Big Tumbling Creek for Twin Hollow Falls
**Start:** Access to scramble down and see Big Falls head-on is from a pull-off on the gravel road. But pay attention, because it's easy to miss. The upper falls is impossible to miss. You can pull right off the road to a perfect gravel viewing area.
**Distance:** Roadside
**Difficulty:** Easy
**Canine compatibility:** N/A

**Trail surface:** N/A
**Hiking time:** 5–10 minutes
**Blaze color:** None
**County:** Russell
**Land status:** Clinch Mountain Wildlife Management Area
**Trail contact:** Department of Game and Inland Fisheries, www.dgif.virginia.gov. Richmond Headquarters: 4010 W. Broad Street, P.O. Box 11104, Richmond, Virginia, 23230
**Maps:** *DeLorme, Virginia Atlas and Gazetteer:* page 22, A2

**Finding the trailhead:** From I-81 use exit 29. Drive north on SR 91 (about 5 miles) until you reach the town of Saltville. In Saltville turn left onto CR 634. At the junction with CR 613, turn left again until you reach CR 747. Turn right onto CR 747 and drive 4.5 miles along this gravel road until you reach Twin Hollow Falls first, then continue up to Big Falls and the Upper Falls. **GPS** for Big Falls: N36 55.931' / W81 49.785'. Twin Hollow: N36 55.851' / W81 49.895'. Upper Falls is 0.2 mile upstream from Big Falls.

*It's easy to miss this delicate double falls on the way to the upper and lower falls on Tumbling Creek.*

# The Hike

If you're like me, you'll fall in love with this creek valley before you ever reach the falls. Once you turn onto CR 747, you'll soon enter the Clinch Mountain WMA, one of many WMAs owned by the Department of Game and Inland Fisheries expressly to offer hunting and fishing opportunities.

When I went in the winter, the yellow metal gate was closed because of snow. When I came back on Memorial Day weekend, the gate was open, and Tumbling Creek was lined with trout anglers.

These are all falls you can see from the road, but you have to take your time with Twin Hollow and Big Falls so you don't drive past them. Twin Hollow can be obscured by vegetation. The winter is probably the best time to get a good look at it. I wasn't able to find a good camera angle to capture it in the late spring, but two mountain creeks come together here to dramatic effect.

*You can pull your car or truck right into the observation area for the upper falls on Tumbling Creek in the Clinch Mountain Wildlife Management Area.*

Just a few hundred feet up the road, there's a pull-off for Big Falls, which you might have to scramble down to get a good look at. It's a powerful cascade, with a promising trout/swimming pool below. The Upper Falls begs to be photographed from the pull-off directly in front of it.

This is definitely a set of falls to package into one trip with the Falls of the Little Stony not too far away.

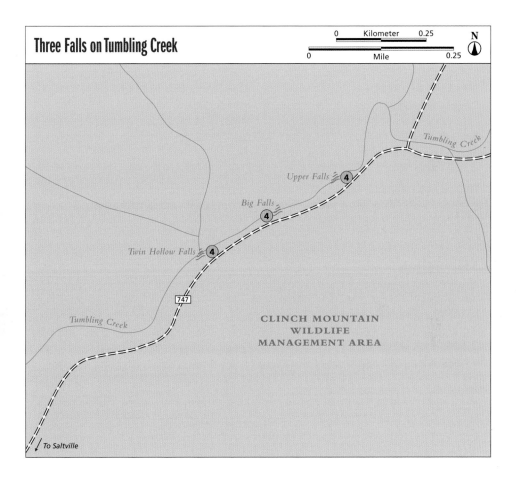

# 5 Big Rock Falls

While Big Rock is more a powerful rapid than an impressive falls, any chance to go to Damascus and hike the Virginia Creeper Trail in the shadow of Mount Rogers is one you should take.

**Height:** A powerful, river-wide drop of 10 feet
**Start:** The Virginia Creeper Trail goes right by the Straight Fork Parking Area. Pick it up at the trailhead.
**Distance:** 2.1 miles out and back
**Difficulty:** Easy/moderate
**Canine compatibility:** Dogs must be on a 6-foot leash on the Virginia Creeper Trail.
**Trail surface:** Wide, hard-packed gravel path
**Hiking time:** About 1 hour

**Blaze color:** None
**County:** Washington
**Land status:** National Forest
**Trail contact:** Jefferson National Forest, (888) 265-0019; www.fs.usda.gov/gwj. Forest Supervisor's Office, 5162 Valleypointe Parkway, Roanoke 24019
**Maps:** *DeLorme, Virginia Atlas and Gazetteer:* page 22, C2

**Finding the trailhead:** Southeast of Damascus you'll find the intersection of US 58 and SR 91. Drive east on US 58 for about 3 miles and turn right into the Straight Fork Parking Area.
**GPS:** N36 38.057' / W81 44.941'

## The Hike

You'll sometimes see this falls referred to as Whitetop Laurel Falls in addition to Big Rock. Whatever you call it, the falls itself is a solid, if unspectacular, entry in this book. What makes this hike worth it is the Virginia Creeper Trail you hike along and the exquisite mountain scenery you take in along the way to and from Big Rock.

Check out the story of the Virginia Creeper Trail in the sidebar. For this hike, start at the Straight Fork Parking Area on the edge of the Jefferson National Forest. Hop on the wide gravel trail and start walking downstream. In the summer you'll have plenty of company from fly fishermen and kayakers on the water and hikers and bikers on the trail. My family and I went in winter and didn't see another soul. Rhododendrons lined the banks of swollen Whitetop Laurel Creek as it rushed toward Damascus and eventually the South Fork Holston River.

You'll know you're closing in on Big Rock Falls when you cross over one of the many old train trestles on the Creeper. The falls will be down to your right. Hop down to river level below the falls, and, if the lighting is right, you'll find a great shot of the falls with the train bridge in the background.

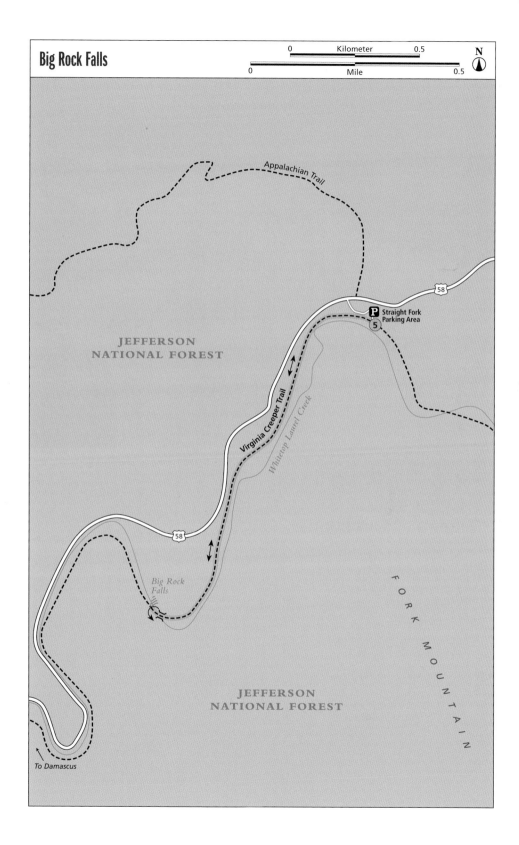

*More gnarly rapid than huge waterfall, Big Rock Falls is nestled along a particularly gorgeous stretch of the Virginia Creeper Trail.*

## Miles and Directions

**0.0** Start at the trailhead in the Straight Fork Parking Area and go right, walking downstream on the Virginia Creeper Trail toward Damascus.

**0.9** Cross an old train bridge just above the falls.

**1.0** Arrive at the falls (GPS: N36 38.057' / W81 44.941'), then retrace your steps to the trailhead.

**2.1** Arrive back at the trailhead.

# VIRGINIA CREEPER TRAIL

The hike to Big Rock Falls near Damascus, Virginia, is the only waterfall hike in this book that takes place solely on a greenway (as opposed to singletrack trail). The easy out-and-back follows Whitetop Laurel Creek on the popular Virginia Creeper Trail.

Even without the waterfall, the Creeper is worth exploring if you find yourself in the southwestern corner of the state. The trail covers 33.4 miles of the former rail bed for the Virginia-Carolina Railroad between downtown Abingdon and the Virginia–North Carolina border 1.1 miles east of the tiny town of Whitetop Station, traveling through Damascus on the way. The trail in its current form was completed in 1984 and is maintained through public-private partnerships between the US Forest Service, the towns of Abingdon and Damascus, and "Creeper Keeper" trail volunteers.

According to vacreepertrail.com, "the locals referred to the train that climbed eastward into the Iron Mountains as the 'Virginia Creeper,' a name taken from the native plant that grows along the route. A steam engine laboring up mountain grades with heavy loads of lumber, iron ore, supplies, and passengers was also a 'Virginia creeper' in every sense of the word."

Today the trail is a tourist draw for the towns and communities along its path. In 2014 the Virginia Creeper Trail was inducted into the Rail-Trail Hall of Fame. For more information on the trail and the amenities along it, check out vacreepertrail.org and vacreepertrail.com.

# 6 Waterfall on Wilson Creek

This hike starts in the forest and then enters a streamside rhododendron tunnel before arriving at the falls. It's more a long cascade over fractured granite than a crashing falls, but the multiple routes the stream takes along the slide offer their own kind of beauty.

**Height:** A sliding cascade of about 30 feet
**Start:** The trailhead is across the street from the Grayson Highlands State Park General Store.
**Distance:** 1.6 miles out and back
**Difficulty:** Moderate
**Canine compatibility:** Dogs must be leashed in all Virginia state parks.
**Trail surface:** Rocky and rooty, bigger boulders near stream

**Hiking time:** About 1 hour
**Blaze color:** Red
**County:** Grayson
**Land status:** Grayson Highlands State Park
**Trail contact:** (276) 579-7092; www.dcr .virginia.gov/state-parks/grayson-highlands .shtml. Park Manager: Grayson Highlands Lane, Mouth of Wilson 24363
**Maps:** *DeLorme, Virginia Atlas and Gazetteer:* page 23, C5

**Finding the trailhead:** From Damascus, take US Route 58 east to SR 362. Turn left on SR 362 into Grayson Highlands State Park. It would probably be a good idea to stop at the visitor center and pick up a map and some other park-related pamphlets. From the park's entrance, follow signs for Wilson Creek and the camping area. Turn right after 3.2 miles, following the signs. In 1.2 miles you'll come to the entrance to the camping area. Park in front of the general store before entering the campground. The trailhead is across the street. **GPS:** N36 38.404' / W81 29.224'

## The Hike

While the Waterfall on Wilson Creek is not the most impressive in this book, the hike is one of my favorites. It starts at the roadside trailhead and eases downhill gradually at first. The surface is rocky and root-strewn and the trail is rather narrow, but it's not particularly difficult to pick one's way down.

After crossing a horse trail, the path through the forest steepens. A half mile into the hike, you'll see a triangular shack below you. In this area the trail surface is almost entirely rocks and a creek seeps its way among them. Keep your eye on the red blazes painted on the trees and you won't get lost.

You should hear Wilson Creek tumbling in the distance by now, and 0.7 mile in you'll see it too. Now the trail heads upstream through a gorgeous rhododendron tunnel. At times it's so close you'll have to duck. There are any number of small falls on the creek down to your right worthy of stopping to enjoy, but the biggest falls is hard to miss. At 0.73 mile the canopy opens up and there's a perfect viewing rock to stand on, lay out a picnic, set up a tripod for pictures—whatever your pleasure.

The falls is more of a slide, but the fractured granite that the creek traverses is beautiful and sends the water rushing in every direction.

# Waterfall on Wilson Creek, Two Falls on Cabin Creek

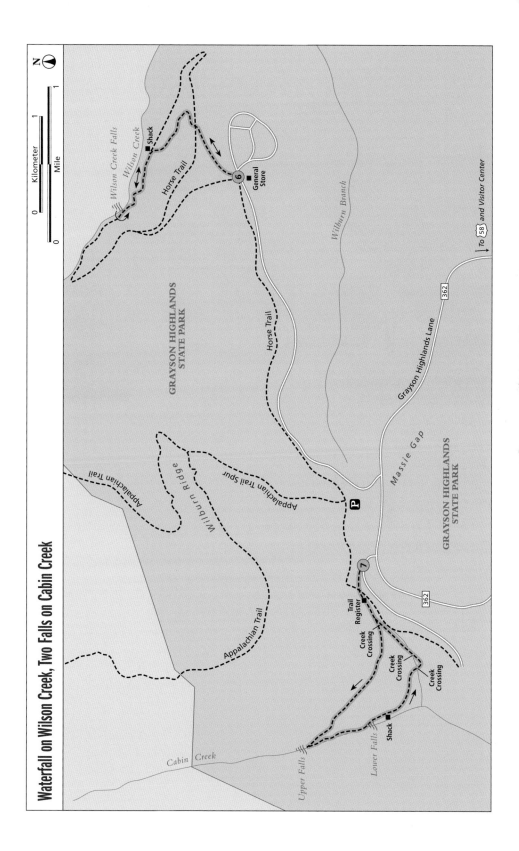

*Take a picnic to the waterfall on Wilson Creek. There's a viewing rock where you can sit and enjoy the rushing water.*

## Miles and Directions

**0.0**   Begin at the trailhead across from the Grayson Highlands State Park General Store.

**0.25**  A wide horse trail crosses the Wilson Creek Trail here. Stay straight, following red blazes.

**0.5**   You'll see a triangular-shaped shack. The trail is not always evident here because of the rocky nature of the trail surface, but just follow the red blazes and you'll be fine.

**0.7**   Arrive at Wilson Creek. Begin following the trail upstream in the rhododendron tunnel. After a few hundred feet, you will arrive at the falls (GPS: N36 38.749' / W81 29.361'). Turn around to retrace your steps.

**1.6**   Arrive back at the trailhead.

# 7 Two Falls on Cabin Creek

This is a great day hike for visitors to Grayson Highlands State Park. In summer the swimming holes along Cabin Creek before the Lower Falls beg to have toes dipped in them. The Upper Falls is impressive too, though somewhat obscured by trees and deadfall.

**See map on page 21.**

**Height:** Lower falls, about 45 feet in 2 sections; upper falls, about 60 feet

**Start:** Begin at the trailhead at the Massie Gap parking lot and follow the yellow blazes.

**Distance:** 1.9 miles in a lollipop shape (1.0 mile to lower Falls; 1.2 miles to upper falls)

**Difficulty:** Moderate

**Canine compatibility:** Dogs must be leashed in all Virginia state parks.

**Trail surface:** Rocky and rooty

**Hiking time:** 1–2 hours

**Blaze color:** Yellow

**County:** Grayson

**Land status:** Grayson Highlands State Park

**Trail contact:** (276) 579-7092; www.dcr .virginia.gov/state-parks/grayson-highlands .shtml. Park Manager: Grayson Highlands Lane, Mouth of Wilson 24363

**Maps:** DeLorme, Virginia Atlas and Gazetteer: page 23, C5

**Finding the trailhead:** From Damascus, take US 58 east to SR 362. Turn left on SR 362 into Grayson Highlands State Park. It would probably be a good idea to stop at the visitor center and pick up a map and some other park-related pamphlets. From the park's entrance, drive 3.5 miles and park on the right at the Massie Gap parking area. The Cabin Creek Trail starts in the middle of the parking area at the obvious trailhead. **GPS:** N36 38.026' / W81 30.577'

## The Hike

While the Wilson Creek waterfall hike on the other side of Grayson Highlands State Park starts in the forest and ends in a rhododendron tunnel, this hike does the opposite. From the Massie Gap parking lot, you'll follow the signs for the yellow-blazed Cabin Creek Trail. Wilburn Ridge, where semi-wild ponies live, will be straight ahead.

The trail will bend off to the left (west), downhill. Soon you'll cross a horse trail and then pass the trail register. Feel free to sign in and check out the hometowns of everyone else who has. Before you reach Cabin Creek and the falls, you'll cross another unnamed creek three times, the first while you're still tucked away in the rhododendron thicket.

A third of a mile into the hike, another trail will split off to the right. That's actually the same trail you're on. The loop starts here. For this hike, stay to left and continue downhill, entering the spruce forest and crossing the stream two more times.

You'll see a triangular shack where the trail reaches Cabin Creek. This is where the hike really gets fun. Follow the trail upstream along the creek, passing many smaller falls and swimming holes. If it's hot out, I'm betting you won't be able to resist going for a dip. But be prepared: The water will be cold! Soon you'll arrive at the lower falls.

*The lower falls on Cabin Creek is the largest in a series of intimate waterfalls along this hike.*

## Miles and Directions

**0.0**  Begin at the trailhead at the Massie Gap parking lot. Follow the yellow blazes.

**0.2**  Cross the horse trail and then the trail register. Sign in if you like.

**0.3**  Arrive at the first small stream crossing.

**0.3**  The lollipop section of trail starts here. You can go left or right. Stay left for this hike.

**0.5**  Cross the stream again. Cross the stream again after a couple hundred feet.

**0.8**  Reach Cabin Creek and the triangular shack, and about 300 feet later, you will arrive at the lower falls. (**Option:** From the Lower Falls, continue about 500 feet along the trail upstream to where the trail makes a sharp switchback to the right. There's a sign here telling you to look for Upper Falls. There's a good observation rock to see the falls from, but there's also a lot of vegetation overhanging the falls. Overall the upper falls isn't as attractive as the lower, but you've got to walk past it on this hike anyway, so it's definitely worth stopping to take in.)

**1.9**  Arrive back at the trailhead.

# GRAYSON HIGHLANDS STATE PARK RHODODENDRON BLOOMS

Because most of the hikes in this book are located in Virginia's various mountain regions, many have surrounding slopes blanketed by different rhododendron species. I was lucky enough to hike a number of these waterfalls in May and June when the rhododendrons were in full bloom. I remember the hike to Crabtree Falls especially for the pink blooms lining the trail, guiding me to the summit. I also hit Apple Orchard Falls at just the right time for a rhododendron show.

On the other hand, I missed out on what many consider Virginia's premier rhododendron performance: Grayson Highlands State Park and the slopes of nearby Mount Rogers.

I hiked the Waterfall on Wilson Creek and Cabin Creek's two falls in the middle of winter in deep snow, but I can just imagine what those hikes would have been like in mid-June, with blooms creating tunnels of color along the creek banks.

If you can time the trip right, hit the two waterfall hikes featured here and then find the Rhododendron Trail. This 2.5-mile path connects Massie Gap with the Appalachian Trail to the north. Many hikers use the Rhododendron Trail to make a 4.3-mile trek to Mount Rogers, which at 5,728 feet is Virginia's highest point.

The Rhododendron Trail connects to the AT spur at Rhododendron Gap. Here you'll pass through the dense thickets of Catawba rhododendron and mountain rosebay that give the trail its name. This area comes alive with color in early to mid-June, and the park probably sees some of its highest visitation because of it. If you happen to get there a little early, you may find mountain laurel and flame azaleas at the lower elevations in May and early June. And if you're late, look for white rhododendrons, called rhododendron maximum, along streams in July.

# 8 Comers Creek Falls

This is a short hike and an easy falls to bag if you're in the Mount Rogers area checking out the falls in Grayson Highlands State Park.

**Height:** About 15 feet
**Start:** There's no official parking area for Comers Creek Falls, but there is room to pull off to the side of the road. The trailhead is well marked.
**Distance:** 0.8 mile out and back
**Difficulty:** Easy
**Canine compatibility:** No leash requirement in general areas of the Jefferson National Forest.
**Trail surface:** Hard-packed dirt, somewhat rocky

**Hiking time:** About 20 minutes
**Blaze color:** Blue, then white on Appalachian Trail
**County:** Smyth
**Land status:** Jefferson National Forest
**Trail contact:** US Forest Service, (888) 265-0019; www.fs.usda.gov/gwj. Forest Supervisor's Office, 5162 Valleypointe Parkway, Roanoke 24019
**Maps:** DeLorme, Virginia Atlas and Gazetteer: page 23, C5

**Finding the trailhead:** From I-81 in Marion take exit 45 and drive south on SR 16. In about 16 miles you'll reach CR 741. Turn right on CR 741 and go less than half a mile to where the road crosses Comers Creek. Be careful here because this trail is an easy one to miss. If you drive more than 0.5 mile, you've gone too far. Park on the side of the road. There is no official parking area. GPS: N36 42.690' / W81 28.455'

## The Hike

Given its location in the greater Damascus / Mount Rogers area, this is a good little falls to add to the list of others in the region. It's nicer than nearby Fox Creek Falls, but like Fox Creek, you probably wouldn't be overjoyed if you drove 2 hours just for this waterfall.

That said, Comers Creek Falls is not a tremendous slouch. It's a good hike to bring kids along on. It's not long or particularly steep, and the bridge across the creek would be a nice place to stop for a picnic lunch. The kids could play in the pool at the base of the falls, while you dip your feet and cool off.

# Comers Creek Falls, Fox Creek Falls

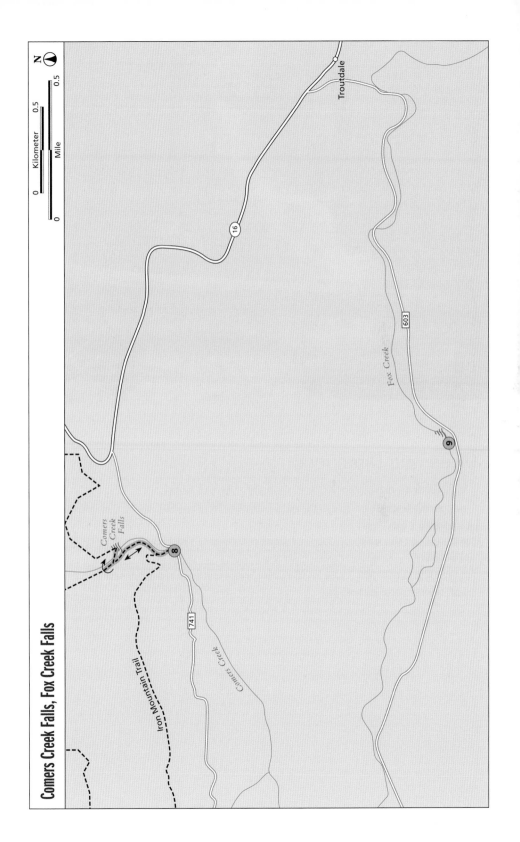

*Comers Creek is a lovely southwest Virginia falls along the Appalachian Trail.*

## Miles and Directions

**0.0**  Follow the old sign for the Comers Creek Trail. It has blue blazes.

**0.2**  Reach the trail junction with the yellow-blazed Iron Mountain Trail. Stay on Comers Creek Trail.

**0.3**  The white-blazed Appalachian Trail comes in. Make a hard right onto it.

**0.4**  Reach the bridge over Comers Creek at the base of the falls on the AT (GPS: N36 42.868' / W81 28.438'), then retrace your steps to the trailhead.

**0.8**  Arrive back at the trailhead.

# 9 Fox Creek Falls

More a slide than a true falls, there is a nice swimming hole at the bottom.

**See map on page 27.**
**Height:** 10 feet
**Start:** From the gravel road, it's really just a scamper down to the falls, not a hike, thus the "roadside" ruling on this one.
**Distance:** Roadside
**Difficulty:** Easy
**Canine compatibility:** N/A
**Trail surface:** N/A
**Hiking time:** 5–10 minutes

**Blaze color:** None
**County:** Grayson
**Land status:** Jefferson National Forest
**Trail contact:** US Forest Service, (888) 265-0019; www.fs.usda.gov/gwj. Forest Supervisor's Office, 5162 Valleypointe Parkway, Roanoke 24019
**Maps:** *DeLorme, Virginia Atlas and Gazetteer:* page 23, C5

**Finding the trailhead:** From I-81 in Marion, take exit 45 and drive south on SR 16. In about 18 miles you'll reach CR 603. Turn right on CR 603 and go less than 2 miles to the pull-off right above the falls. Take the obvious path just a few feet down to the creek. **GPS:** N36 41.823' / W81 27.989'

*Maybe not a destination falls by itself, Fox Creek Falls is, nevertheless, one to include if you're hiking multiple waterfalls in the area.*

# The Hike

It's with falls like Fox Creek where we start getting into definitions. Is this really a falls? Is it a slide? Even calling it a cascade might be generous. It's not tall, but it's not just a trickle. There's usually plenty of water in the stream. And there are other things to recommend Fox Creek Falls: It's in a particularly fetching bend of the creek, and there is a nice swimming area below it.

So, whatever you do, don't seek out Fox Creek Falls if you're in search of a mind-blowing Virginia waterfall experience. Instead, pair it with other area falls, especially Comers Creek. And do sit awhile on a rock below the falls and bathe in the serenity that even a slide of this size offers.

## THE CLINCH RIVER

As you drive the back roads of southwestern Virginia in search of waterfalls, you'll cross and recross the Clinch River. Maybe you'll note its natural beauty, but you might not know that the Clinch isn't just any run-of-the-mill waterway.

The Clinch is ecologically significant enough that the Nature Conservancy has a program—the Clinch Valley Program—dedicated exclusively to its preservation. The Clinch, along with the neighboring Powell and Holston Rivers, according to the Nature Conservancy, "harbor the nation's highest concentrations of globally rare and imperiled fish and freshwater mussels."

According to the Virginia Department of Game and Inland Fisheries, "the Clinch supports a unique assemblage of aquatic life. The river is home to about 50 species of mussels, which is more than any other river in the world, and over 100 species of non-game fish—minnows and darters that sport brilliant colors and play a vital role in the survival of other fish and mussel species. A variety of sport fish—like trout and smallmouth bass—also makes the Clinch a great destination for anglers."

Maybe the most charismatic resident of the Clinch is the eastern hellbender, a large, stout-bodied, fully aquatic salamander that can grow to be over a foot long. Hellbenders are known to live to thirty years in the wild and over fifty years in captivity, and because of their preference for clean streams and rivers, hellbenders serve as indicators of stream health. The presence of young and adult hellbenders is synonymous with good water quality. In Virginia eastern hellbenders only exist in the Clinch, Powell, and Holston Rivers, as well as a portion of the New River.

# 10 Waterfall on Garrett Creek

This is an easy and striking falls to add to a trip into this area, and one of the few private property falls of which you can get good pictures from the road.

**Height:** 45 feet
**Start:** Hop out of your car on the gravel road. It's remote. You should have it to yourself.
**Distance:** Roadside
**Difficulty:** Easy
**Canine compatibility:** N/A
**Trail surface:** N/A
**Hiking time:** N/A

**Blaze color:** None
**County:** Washington
**Land status:** On private property, but viewed from public land
**Trail contact:** N/A
**Maps:** *DeLorme, Virginia Atlas and Gazetteer:* page 21, B7

**Finding the trailhead:** Start in Abingdon and drive north on US 19/US Alt. 58. Just before crossing the North Fork Holston River, turn left on gravel CR 611. Drive 2 miles until you see the obvious waterfall on the right. **GPS:** N36 46.253' / W82 54.182'

*View this private property waterfall from the public gravel road next to it.*

# The Hike

The number of waterfalls on private property in Virginia is staggering. If you had access and could write a book just on those, you might have more entries than there are in this book. Unfortunately, most private property falls are off-limits. The Waterfall on Garrett Creek, happily, isn't one of them. From the road you can hop out of your car, set up a tripod on the gravel road, and snap a few pics. You'll have a better view in the winter, but even when the leaves are on the trees, you'll still have a mostly unobscured look at the cascade.

Is this falls worthy of a special trip? Probably not, but Tank Hollow Falls and Big Falls on Big Cedar Creek are in the area (and the Falls of the Little Stony aren't too far away). It's worth adding to the list if you're headed here to see those.

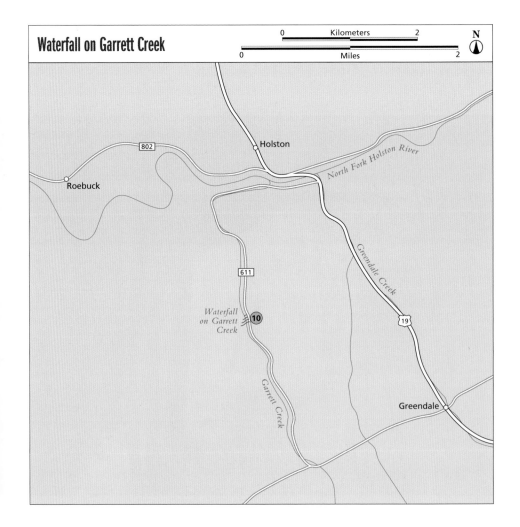

Waterfall on Garrett Creek

# 11 Falls of Dismal

This falls offers multiple cascades over a series of ledges with a large swimming hole at the bottom. Plan a picnic, swim, sit on the rocks. Definitely spend some time here. This one is a southwest Virginia keeper.

**Height:** A series of ledges about 15 feet
**Start:** The pull-off on the side of the road isn't much, and there's no real trailhead because there's no real trail. But the sign for "Dismal Falls" should be all the clue you need.
**Distance:** 0.1 mile out and back
**Difficulty:** Easy
**Canine compatibility:** There is no leash requirement in general areas of the Jefferson National Forest.
**Trail surface:** Loose dirt

**Hiking time:** About 5 minutes
**Blaze color:** None
**County:** Bland
**Land status:** Jefferson National Forest
**Trail contact:** US Forest Service, (888) 265-0019; www.fs.usda.gov/gwj. Forest Supervisor's Office, 5162 Valleypointe Parkway, Roanoke 24019
**Maps:** DeLorme, Virginia Atlas and Gazetteer: page 40, C2

**Finding the trailhead:** From I-77 in the town of Bland, head east on SR 42 for about 14 miles. Turn left on CR 606 and drive just under a mile to CR 671. Turn right on CR 671 and stay on it for just under a mile. You'll see a pull-off on the right with a sign that says "Dismal Falls." **GPS:** N37 11.109' / W80 54.094'

## The Hike

The sign at the roadside says "Dismal Falls," but everywhere else I've seen it referenced, it's "Falls of Dismal." I went with Falls of Dismal because it seemed to have more panache. Whatever you call it, this waterfall is great in every way except height and hike length. If you're looking for a strenuous hike to a big drop, try the not-too-distant Cascades.

Falls of Dismal is a pretty little series of falls over flat ledges on Dismal Creek (**Note:** It's not actually on Pearis Thompson Branch, as some maps show). The hike is a little over 100 yards round-trip, so you can easily pack a lunch and hang out on the many rocks both above and below the falls. The water will be at least cool, if not always cold, year-round, but if it's hot out, there's a large swimming hole at the base that's just begging to be relaxed in. Put this on the list of great Virginia waterfalls for families.

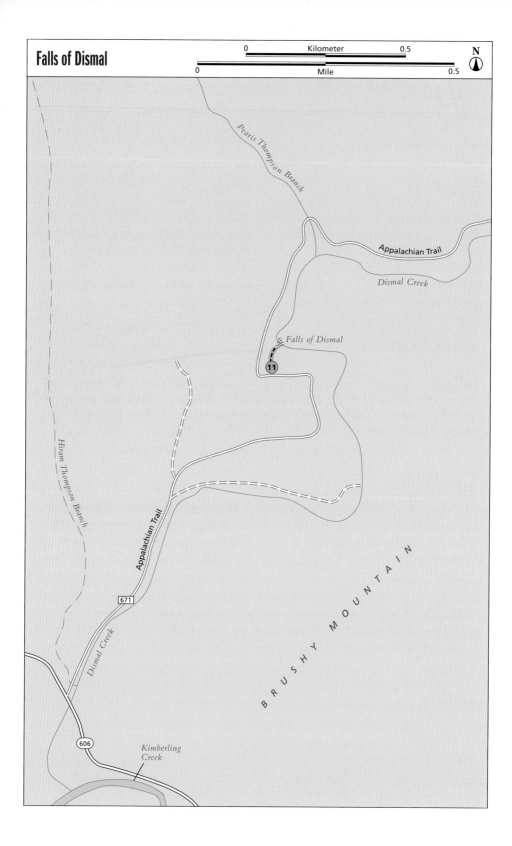

**Falls of Dismal**

Kilometer

0            0.5

Mile

0            0.5

N

Pearis Thompson Branch

Appalachian Trail

Dismal Creek

Falls of Dismal

11

Hiram Thompson Branch

Appalachian Trail

671

Dismal Creek

BRUSHY MOUNTAIN

606

Kimberling Creek

*The stairstep pattern of the Falls of Dismal and the deep swimming hole below make this a must-see Virginia waterfall.*

## Miles and Directions

**0.0**   From the pull-off on the side of CR 671, where the sign says "Dismal Falls," hike down the obvious trail to the base of the falls (GPS: N37 11.141' / W80 54.099').

**0.05** Arrive at the base of the falls, then retrace your steps.

**0.1**   Return to the trailhead.

# Valley and Ridge

Like "Piedmont," the term "Valley and Ridge" refers to a physiographic province. The Valley and Ridge is characterized by long parallel ridges and valleys with folded sedimentary rock below them (the valleys) and inside them (the ridges) that eroded at different rates, thus the valleys and ridges.

You'd think it was those ridges that account for waterfalls in this section, but that's not always the case. The Valley and Ridge section also boasts a number of "travertine falls," waterfalls that form as calcium carbonate in spring water comes out of solution and is deposited as limestone rock, building up and eventually creating a waterfall. Falling Spring Falls, the Waterfall at Falls Ridge, Cypress Falls, and the waterfall on a tributary of the Middle River are all travertine falls, and they make for some nice variety when searching out Virginia's falls.

For Virginia waterfall seekers in the Valley and Ridge, I-81 is your all-access pass. From the Waterfall at Falls Ridge, near Blacksburg, to the waterfall that flows from an unnamed tributary into the Middle River north of Staunton, you're never far from I-81 when you're hunting cataracts in this region. I'm not sure there's a single waterfall in the Valley and Ridge that is more than 30 minutes from I-81. That means you can often hit multiple falls in a day, even when they include challenging hikes.

The Valley and Ridge also features some pretty back roads and towns that make waterfall hounding here a delight. Lexington, Staunton, Harrisonburg, and Blacksburg, as well as the larger Roanoke, are all destinations by themselves, with quaint shops and vibrant restaurants along lovely main streets. Definitely take your time in the Valley and Ridge and absorb all the area has to offer.

# 12 Waterfall at Falls Ridge

This is one of a few waterfalls in Virginia—and probably the most unusual looking of them—formed from the buildup of travertine over millions of years.

**Height:** 70 feet
**Start:** Trailhead is at the end of the gravel lot with the grassy field stretching out behind it. The trail winds through that field.
**Distance:** 0.6 mile out and back
**Difficulty:** Easy
**Canine compatibility:** Dogs are not allowed on any Nature Conservancy property.
**Trail surface:** Hard-packed dirt

**Hiking time:** About 15 minutes
**Blaze color:** None
**County:** Montgomery
**Land status:** Nature Conservancy property
**Trail contact:** Nature Conservancy; nature.org (search "Falls Ridge"). The Nature Conservancy, 490 Westfield Road, Charlottesville 22901
**Maps:** DeLorme, Virginia Atlas and Gazetteer: page 41, C7

**Finding the trailhead:** From I-81 south of Roanoke, take CR 603 (North Fork Road) west at exit 128. Go 7 miles on CR 603 and then turn onto a private, wooden bridge over the North Fork Roanoke River. You'll pass a couple of similar bridges before you get to the correct bridge, but don't turn onto them. You'll know you're on the correct bridge because after crossing the bridge, you'll almost immediately cross a set of train tracks. Take a left after the tracks. Go 0.3 mile stay left at the fork and park in the gravel lot with Nature Conservancy signage and the obvious trailhead in front of you. **GPS:** N37 11.589' / W80 19.299'

## The Hike

Like many Nature Conservancy properties in Virginia, the Falls Ridge Preserve is not easy to find—you'll rarely see road signs until you reach an actual preserve—but once you find it, the trails are well marked and easy to navigate.

The Waterfall at Falls Ridge is notable not so much for the hike to it—that's short, flat, and straight—but for the falls itself. Like a few others in this book, it's a travertine falls, where minerals, like calcium carbonate, dissolved in the water precipitate upon the rocks and build them up. According the Nature Conservancy website, "over thousands of years, the build-up of calcium carbonate steepened the stream's gradient and slowly created both the waterfall and one of the largest known exposed travertine deposits."

As previously mentioned, there are other travertine falls in Virginia, most notably Falling Spring Falls.

But the Waterfall at Falls Ridge is different in appearance than those or any other falls in the state. The water crashes over rocks that don't look like rocks—they look like giant boulders of mud. You'll swear they're mud until you touch them and realize they're as hard as any other rock. It's quite a fascinating place. But remember, the preserve also is home to a number of rare plant species, so stay on the trail and take only pictures.

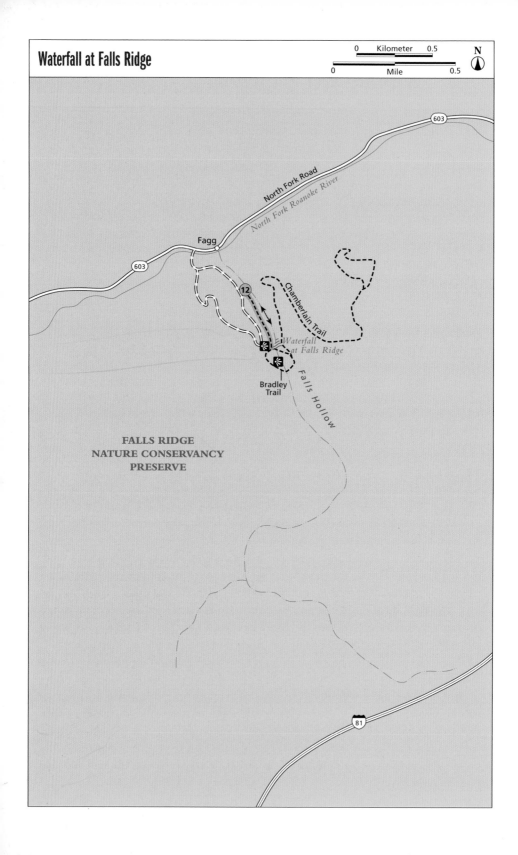

# Waterfall at Falls Ridge

*Could this be the strangest looking waterfall in the state?*

## Miles and Directions

**0.0**   Begin at the trailhead at the gravel lot. The trail is not blazed, but it is obvious as it goes through the grassy field in front of you.

**0.3**   Arrive at the base of the falls (GPS: N37 11.381' / W80 19.198), then retrace your steps to the trailhead.

**0.6**   Arrive back at the trailhead.

# 13 The Cascades

Some experiences in life just never live up to their significant hype. Happily, hiking to the Cascades is not one of those. You may have heard about the Cascades from lots of friends. You may hike alongside dozens of people on the way there. You may find even more people gaping at the base of the falls. No matter: The Cascades will blow you away.

**Height:** 65 feet
**Start:** The trailhead is at the far end of the parking lot from where you enter. It's to the right of the restroom facilities.
**Distance:** 4.0 miles out and back or loop
**Difficulty:** Strenuous
**Canine compatibility:** There is no leash requirement in general areas of the Jefferson National Forest.
**Trail surface:** Rocky, rooty singletrack

**Hiking time:** 1–2 hours
**Blaze color:** None
**County:** Giles
**Land status:** Jefferson National Forest
**Trail contact:** US Forest Service, (888) 265-0019; www.fs.usda.gov/gwj. Forest Supervisor's Office, 5162 Valleypointe Parkway, Roanoke 24019
**Maps:** *DeLorme, Virginia Atlas and Gazetteer:* page 41, B5

**Finding the trailhead:** In Blacksburg take US 460 west for 15 miles to the town of Pembroke. Go right on CR 623 and drive 3.5 miles to the parking lot for the Cascades Day-Use Area.
**GPS:** N37 21.226' / W80 35.937'

## The Hike

The 4-mile hike to and from the Cascades can be done as an out-and-back on the same singletrack or as a loop hike, where you hike the singletrack one way and a gravel fire road the other. Either way the distance is the same: The singletrack hugs Little Stony Creek, offering gorgeous vantages the entire way, the fire road is better for pushing strollers and for hikers who prefer a flat path, but the views are not as good.

If you're going to make the trip to the Cascades, and you're physically able, you owe it to yourself to at least hike to the falls on the rocky singletrack that stays right next to the creek. The Little Stony cuts a sometimes-narrow gorge between Butt and Doe Mountains, and the hike alone would be worth it even if it didn't end at one of the top three waterfalls in the state. There are giant boulders hanging above gin-clear pools and mini-waterfalls all along the creek's course. Rock slides are evident in a couple of places. There is even another trickle of a waterfall that drops directly into the Little Stony near the top. But you'll miss all that if you take the fire road.

The combined hike/waterfall Cascades experience won't disappoint, no matter how much someone has built it up. If you go in summer, you'll pass dozens of hikers

*If you could only hike one Virginia waterfall, this would have to be on your short list. Just don't expect to be alone on the hike or at the falls.*

on the trail. If you go in winter, there'll be far fewer, but you probably won't be alone. One nice thing is that the area around the waterfall is huge, and there are plenty of rocks for people to spread out on.

The Cascades is your quintessential amphitheater falls, only it's taller and wider than most. And the swimming hole below it is bigger than any other I can think of in the state.

If you've researched the Cascades, you may have come across reports about another significant waterfall above it. Those reports are true. It exists, but when I hiked the Cascades, there was a National Forest ranger standing in the exact spot where you'd need to go to scramble up and around the main falls to reach the upper falls. He told me about it, and then he showed me the sign warning people not to scramble up that way. On another day things might have been different, but I just wasn't meant to see the upper Cascades on that day.

In any event, put the Cascades on your Virginia waterfalls bucket list. It is a true wonder.

# The Cascades

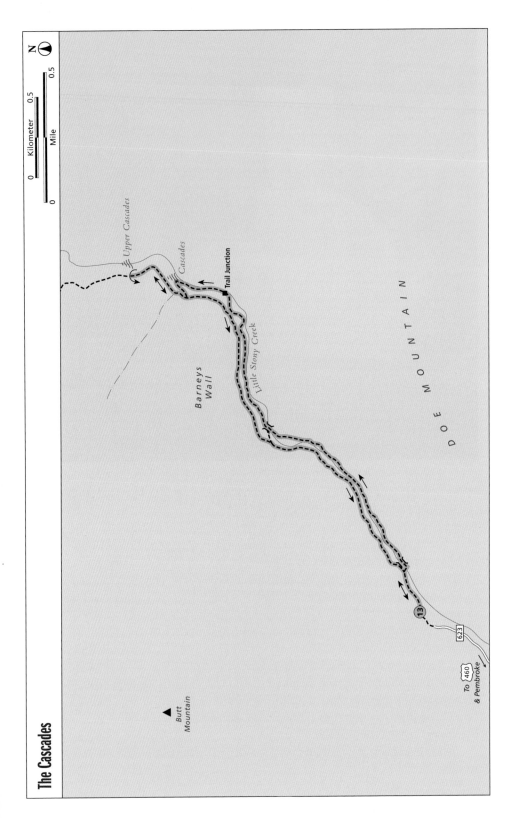

# Miles and Directions

**0.0** Begin hiking from the trailhead at the end of the parking lot.

**0.1** Choose the singletrack option, which stays right along Little Stony Creek, and cross the creek over a bridge.

**1.0** Cross back over the creek on another bridge.

**1.4** Check out the small falls across the creek that drops directly into the Little Stony.

**2.0** Arrive at a huge pool at the base of the falls (GPS: N37 22.071' / W80 34.514'). Climb the stairs above the falls observation area and take the fire road back to the trailhead. (*Option:* Retrace your steps, returning on the same path.)

**4.0** Arrive back at the trailhead.

# WHAT IS TRAVERTINE?

Perhaps by now you've paged through, or been to, enough of these falls to notice a subset called travertine falls. These are some of my favorites in Virginia because they tend to occur in places— i.e., not actually along mountain ranges—and look different than most other cataracts.

The Waterfall at Falls Ridge, Cypress Falls, and the insanely photogenic Falling Springs Falls (to name three) were all formed in similar ways: through the precipitation of travertine, a kind of limestone, out of solution. In all three places natural springs carry water supercharged with calcium carbonate, the active ingredient in travertine limestone.

This material comes out of that water/calcium carbonate solution (see page 36) and is deposited over time. So the streams essentially build the waterfall they eventually tumble over as opposed to cutting it through bedrock. Such waterfalls are described by geologists as a living phenomenon because they are continuously rebuilt by the sediments in spring water. Yellowstone National Park probably has the most well-known travertine deposits in America, where the geothermal springs are rich in the limestone variety.

# 14 Roaring Run Falls

This short hike offers a few inviting rock slides in addition to the final cascade. It's a popular place with whitewater boaters after heavy rains and with everyone else the rest of the year due to the ease in reaching it.

**Height:** About 40 feet
**Start:** The trailhead resides at the far end of the parking area near the restrooms.
**Distance:** 1.3 miles out and back
**Difficulty:** Easy/moderate
**Canine compatibility:** Dogs are allowed off-leash in national forests.
**Trail surface:** Sometimes rocky and rooty, but not steep
**Hiking time:** About 40 minutes

**Blaze color:** None, but trail has good signage
**County:** Botetourt
**Land status:** National Forest
**Trail contact:** Jefferson National Forest, (888) 265-0019; www.fs.usda.gov/gwj. Forest Supervisor's Office, 5162 Valleypointe Parkway, Roanoke 24019
**Maps:** *DeLorme, Virginia Atlas and Gazetteer:* page 52, C3

**Finding the trailhead:** From I-81 north of Roanoke, take exit 150 and get on US 220 north. Drive to Eagle Rock, then turn left on CR 615. Stay on CR 615 for 5.5 miles, then turn right onto CR 621. In just under a mile, you'll see a Jefferson National Forest "Historical Site" sign. Turn left there and it is 0.25 mile to the parking area. **GPS:** N37 42.404' / W79 53.589'

## The Hike

This hike/falls combo packs a lot of punch for not being very long (the hike) or high (the falls). Its lack of elevation change and trailhead amenities make it a good choice for family outings. It also offers a few impressive, perfectly flat rock slides before you reach the actual falls. On a Memorial Day hike, I saw a number of high school–age kids taking advantage of the best of those slides and the pool below it.

The trail you hike is officially the Roaring Run National Recreation Trail, and the Forest Service keeps it well maintained and well signed. Even without this book, it would be impossible to get lost on this hike. If you want to know why this area is considered a historic site, on your way back from the falls, take the "Woodland Trail" back to the parking area. Along the way you'll pass the ruins of the old Roaring Run iron furnace.

As for the falls itself, it won't overpower you with its height—it might be 35 to 40 feet—but there's room to swim at the bottom, and there are lots of picnic spots. Because of its easy accessibility, don't expect to have it to yourself, except maybe in winter.

*Be careful if you venture to the top of this waterfall. The rocks can be more slick than they appear.*

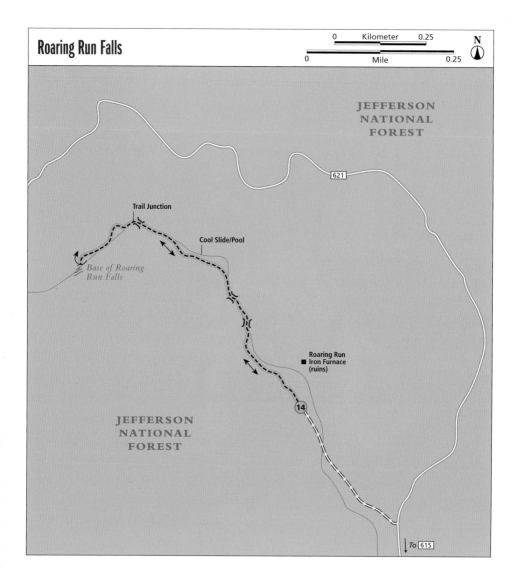

## Miles and Directions

**0.0** The streamside trail begins past the trail kiosk to the left of the restrooms.

**0.2** Cross a wooden bridge over the Roaring Run, then recross the stream on another wooden bridge a few hundred feet later.

**0.5** Cross another bridge, then come to the junction where the well-signed Woodland Trail splits off.

**0.7** Arrive at the base of the falls (GPS: N37 42.618' / W79 53.998'), then retrace your steps to the trailhead.

**1.3** Arrive back at the trailhead.

# 15  Falling Spring Falls

One of the most historic waterfalls in the state—Thomas Jefferson wrote about it in his *Notes on the State of Virginia*—this one is also a geologic oddity.

**Height:** 80 feet
**Start:** From the parking area, check out the information kiosk, then walk about 10 yards on the paved path to the viewing area.
**Distance:** Roadside
**Difficulty:** Easy
**Canine compatibility:** N/A
**Trail surface:** N/A
**Hiking time:** 5-10 minutes
**Blaze color:** None

**County:** Alleghany
**Land status:** State owned
**Trail contact:** Virginia Department of Conservation and Recreation, (804) 786-7951; http://www.dcr.virginia.gov. Division of Natural Heritage, 600 E. Main Street, Richmond 23219
**Maps:** *DeLorme, Virginia Atlas and Gazetteer:* page 52, B3

**Finding the trailhead:** From I-64, take exit 16 onto US 220 north. Drive nearly 10 miles and you'll see the falls, then the parking area, on the left. **GPS:** N37 52.032' / W79 56.879'

## The Hike

It's not exactly clear why Thomas Jefferson, when he mentioned Falling Spring Falls in 1781 in his writings, described it as falling "over a rock 200 feet into the valley below."

The falls is more like an 80-foot drop, but it is, nevertheless, very impressive. Virginia doesn't have very many sheer-drop falls with this much height, and most of them are in the Shenandoah National Park area. This one seems to come out of nowhere, making it that much more impressive.

In fact, where it comes from (according to signage at the parking area) is from a spring in Warm River Cave about a mile north.

*Thomas Jefferson once marveled at the grandeur of Falling Spring Falls, a true Virginia classic.*

There "warm thermal spring water and a cold stream of shallow groundwater mix in the cave before surfacing" as Falling Spring Creek. "The water is supersaturated carbonate that forms travertine—a form of limestone—at the base of the falls."

Even without a hike to boost its cred, Falling Spring Falls is a gorgeous sight and well worth the trip to this area in far-western Virginia.

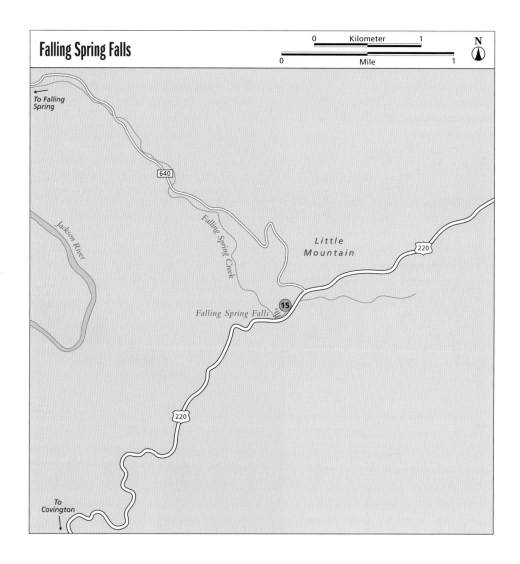

# 16 Stony Run Falls

While not a stunner, this falls is a nice excuse for a woodland hike in Douthat State Park. And it's easily included in a loop hike that includes Blue Suck Falls, Douthat's other worthy cascade.

**Height:** 20 feet over a set of slides
**Start:** The Stony Run Trailhead is right next to where you park. There's nowhere else to go from this gravel lot.
**Distance:** 3.5 miles out and back
**Difficulty:** Moderate
**Canine compatibility:** Dogs must be leashed in all Virginia state parks.
**Trail surface:** Wide, hard-packed dirt with some rocky sections

**Hiking time:** 1–2 hours
**Blaze color:** Orange
**County:** Alleghany
**Land status:** Douthat State Park
**Trail contact:** (540) 862-8100; www.dcr .virginia.gov/state-parks/douthat.shtml. Park Manager: 14239 Douthat State Park Road, Millboro 24460
**Maps:** *DeLorme, Virginia Atlas and Gazetteer:* page 53, A5

**Finding the trailhead:** From I-64 take CR 629 north (exit 27) 5 miles to Douthat State Park. You'll see the signs on your left for the Stony Run Trail and small gravel parking area. Don't forget to pay the parking fee at the visitor center farther up the road. **GPS:** N37 53.275' / W79 48.221'

## The Hike

If you've looked at the Miles and Directions for this hike, you'll see many creek crossings, maybe the most of any hike in this book. Not to fear. Unless you're hiking just after a gully washer, you should be able to hop rocks safely at each crossing. And that will be part of the fun.

This is one of those falls where the hike is probably more enjoyable than the experience at the falls itself. Rhododendrons create a neat tunnel effect at Stony Run Falls, but they also make it nearly impossible to get a good picture. Still, you'll find a series of slides and a few small pools at Stony Run Falls. Dip your feet, eat a sandwich, then head back in search of everything else Douthat State Park has to offer.

*Could this be a trail marker tree? Trail marker trees are hardwoods that have been shaped by humans in the past to mark a trail.*

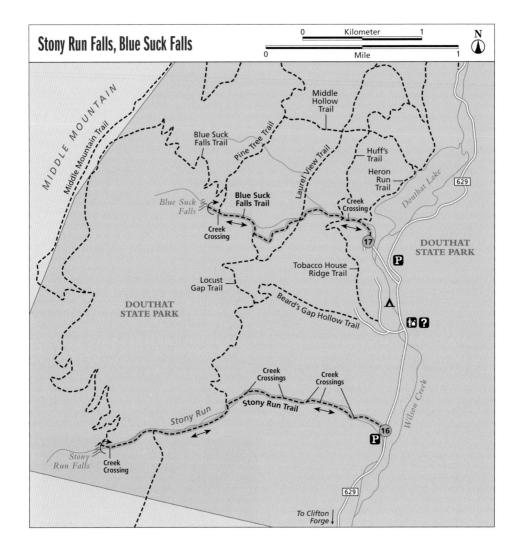

## Stony Run Falls, Blue Suck Falls

## Miles and Directions

**0.0** Begin hiking on well-marked, orange-blazed Stony Run Trail.

**0.2** Cross Stony Run for the first of many times.

**0.4** Reach creek crossing number two, then number three on a side creek immediately after number two.

**0.5** Reach creek crossing number four.

**0.6** Reach creek crossing number five.

**0.7** Observe the cool "trail tree" pointing the way forward, then, at about 0.8 mile, creek crossing number six crosses a side creek.

**0.9** The trail junction with Locust Gap Trail comes in on the right. Stay on Stony Run Trail. Then creek crossing number seven appears almost immediately.

**1.4** An equestrian trail enters from the left.

**1.7** Reach creek crossing number eight, then stay left on the side trail along Stony Run. That will take you to the base of the falls.

**1.8** Arrive at the base of the falls (GPS: N37 53.207' / W79 49.846').

**3.5** Arrive back at the trailhead.

# DOUTHAT STATE PARK AND THE CCC

On June 15, 1936, Virginia became the first state to open an entire park system on the same day. Six parks came online that day, including Douthat State Park, where Blue Suck Falls and Stony Run Falls are located.

Douthat remains one of Virginia's most popular state parks this day largely because of its stunning natural beauty and rugged location in the Allegheny Mountains, but its history is also worth noting.

The Douthat Land Company—a consortium of Virginia businessmen, donated the initial 1,920 acres of the present-day, now-4,500-acre park. The rest of the land was purchased with a portion of the $50,000 in funds allocated by the General Assembly in 1933 for parkland acquisition. The establishment of the Civilian Conservation Corps (CCC) as part of the emergency Conservation Works by President Franklin D. Roosevelt in 1933 provided the means for development of the park.

An estimated 600 men lived and worked at the three camps responsible for building Douthat's facilities. Between 1933 and 1942, these men cleared trails and built a dam and spillway, cabins, a restaurant, an information center, the superintendent's residence, a swimming beach, picnic areas and a maintenance building, as well as hand-wrought iron hardware and light fixtures.

Visitors can see the incredible craftsmanship of CCC workers everywhere in Douthat, maybe most notably at the gorgeous two-tiered dam and spillway, but also in the numerous hand-hewn log cabins and lodges. What's amazing about the built features of Douthat is that, like its natural ones, they have remained virtually unchanged since their construction decades ago.

# 17 Blue Suck Falls

This great hike in Douthat State Park should definitely be coupled with nearby Stony Run Falls, either as a separate hike or a loop. And about that name: No one at the state park that I talked to knew where the name came from or how long the waterfall has been called that. The best guess the park information person could muster is that a "suck" was local usage for a small stream years ago. That could be true, but I can't find any other "sucks" on a map of the area. Blue Suck Falls: one of a kind!

**See map on page 50.**

**Height:** Series of steep but small cascades totaling 35–40 feet

**Start:** The trailhead, with a detailed map, is at the end of the parking lot nearest Douthat Lake.

**Distance:** 2.3 miles out and back

**Difficulty:** Moderate

**Canine compatibility:** Dogs must be leashed.

**Trail surface:** Rocky singletrack

**Hiking time:** 1–2 hours

**Blaze color:** Blue

**County:** Alleghany

**Land status:** Douthat State Park

**Trail contact:** (540) 862-8100; http://www
.dcr.virginia.gov/state-parks/douthat.shtml.
Park Manager: 14239 Douthat State Park
Road, Millboro 24460

**Maps:** *DeLorme, Virginia Atlas and Gazetteer:* page 53, A5

**Finding the trailhead:** From I-64 take CR 629 north (exit 27) 5 miles to Douthat State Park. Pass the signs for the Stony Run Trail on your left, and don't forget to pay the parking fee at the visitor center farther up the road. Once you do that, drive north 0.3 mile on CR 629 and turn left into the parking area at the base of Douthat Lake. You'll have to cross Wilson Creek to get there. Look for the obvious trailhead signage. **GPS:** N37 54.101' / W79 48.315'

## The Hike

Like with its Douthat State Park sister falls—Stony Run Falls—the Blue Suck Falls experience is as much about the hike as it is the waterfall. In fact, with either it's best to go after a good rain. But no matter when you go to Blue Suck, you'll enjoy the time spent reaching it.

When I went in the winter, the park had recently conducted a controlled burn over dozens of acres of hardwood forest on both sides of the trail. It made for some interesting sights (and smells), and the results of this burn will probably be visible for at least a few more years. The hike has numerous other trails entering at different points, but the signage is top-notch. You'll never wonder whether you're going the right way.

You can hike Stony Run Falls and Blue Suck Falls together by using the Locust Gap Trail to link the two. Pick up a map at the park visitor center to explore that possibility.

*Blue Suck Falls is the destination of one of two challenging waterfall hikes in the popular Douthat State Park.*

## Miles and Directions

**0.0** Follow blue blazes (and good signage) on Blue Suck Falls Trail.

**0.1** Heron Run Trail joins from the right. Tobacco House Ridge Trail comes in from the left a couple hundred feet later, then you cross a creek almost immediately.

**0.3** Huff's Trail joins from the right.

**0.5** Laurel View Trail comes in from the right, then there's another creek crossing.

**0.8** Locust Gap Trail comes in from the left.

**1.0** The trail enters Blue Suck Run for a bit as you rock-hop through the middle.

**1.2** Arrive at the base of the falls, where the trail does a switchback (GPS: N37 54.267' / W79 49.234'). Then retrace your steps to the trailhead.

**2.3** Arrive back at the trailhead.

# 18 Falls on Tributary to Middle River

Any time you've got a creek falling directly into a river, you're sure to have a winner. That's the case here, and it's worth braving the camping hordes to see.

**Height:** 25 feet
**Start:** The view of the falls across the Middle River is maybe 100 yards south of the campground headquarters.
**Distance:** N/A
**Difficulty:** Easy
**Canine compatibility:** N/A
**Trail surface:** N/A
**Hiking time:** 5-10 minutes

**Blaze color:** None
**County:** Augusta
**Land status:** Private campground
**Trail contact:** Shenandoah Valley Campground, (540) 248-CAMP; campingisfun.com. Bald Rock Road, Verona 24482
**Maps:** DeLorme, Virginia Atlas and Gazetteer: page 66, C3

**Finding the trailhead:** Take exit 227 off I-81 in Staunton and drive west on CR 612. Go just under a mile and turn right, heading north on US 11. Drive another 0.5 mile and turn left on CR 781. In 1 mile you'll see signs to turn left into the entrance for the Shenandoah Valley Campground. If you follow the main road that parallels the Middle River, you'll pass the campground headquarters and loop around to the falls in about 100 yards. **GPS:** N38 13.262' / W79 00.996'

*Stay at the Shenandoah Valley Campground and you can frolic in the Middle River beneath this falls.*

## The Hike

Tiny Falling Spring Run slides over travertine here, creating a gorgeous cascade across the river from the private campground. When my family and I arrived, we simply asked the lady at the front desk if it was OK to go take some pictures of the falls even if we weren't staying at the campground. She was fine with it. I don't see why she wouldn't say the same to you. Better yet, book a stay at the campground far enough in advance and maybe you could secure the campsite directly opposite this falls. Then you could really spend some time investigating it.

If you happen to be in the Staunton area, this cascade is well worth checking out. There are only a handful of falls in Virginia where one body of water falls directly into another. Why not collect them all? (But keep in mind that the campground is usually open only from April to the end of October.)

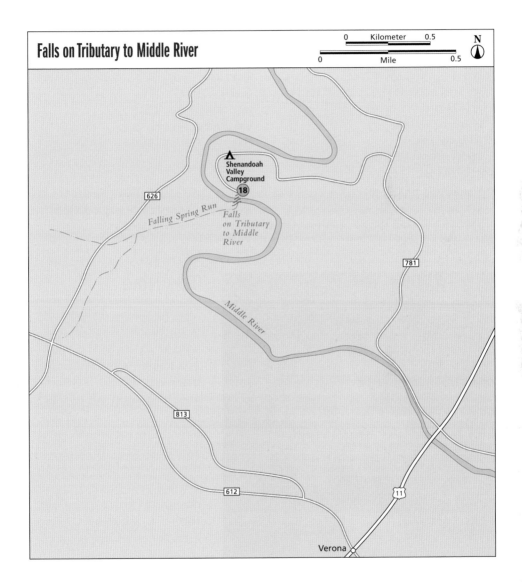

Falls on Tributary to Middle River

# 19 Cypress Falls

You wouldn't expect Cypress Falls to be where it is, sitting in the South River Valley. And in summer, when the trees are fully leafed out, you could easily miss it if you don't know what to look for.

**Height:** 25 feet
**Start:** There's room to pull off on the side of CR 608 directly across from Cypress Falls. You'll see an obvious trail to the river that years of waterfall gawkers have worn down.
**Distance:** Roadside
**Difficulty:** Easy
**Canine compatibility:** N/A

**Trail surface:** N/A
**Hiking time:** N/A
**Blaze color:** None
**County:** Augusta
**Land status:** Private property
**Trail contact:** None
**Maps:** *DeLorme, Virginia Atlas and Gazetteer:* page 54, B1

**Finding the trailhead:** From Lexington drive north on US 11 for approximately 3.5 miles. Turn right on CR 716 (Timber Ridge Road) and go south for 3 miles. Turn right on CR 608 and drive less than a mile. The falls will be on your right. **GPS:** N37 47.920' / W79 20.082'

*Cypress Falls seems to emerge magically from the forest above.*

## The Hike

Like the falls on the tributary to the Middle River 40 minutes north of here, Cypress Falls features water falling over travertine—a kind of limestone that forms out of solution in water, often near hot springs. That's why, in Virginia and elsewhere, you'll often see travertine waterfalls in places that don't have much elevation change. And like its cousin falls north of Staunton, Cypress Falls is especially beautiful because it features one watercourse—Sheep Creek—falling directly into another—the South River. The falls itself has multiple ledges and disappears at the top into the forest.

When you pull off to the side of the road, you may see some "Posted" signs in the area, but when I visited, there were none immediately opposite the falls. Nevertheless, it's probably best to think of this as a winter waterfall. With the leaves off the roadside trees and shrubs, you'll have a clear view from CR 608 and you won't have to trespass to see this quite beautiful, and surprising, falls.

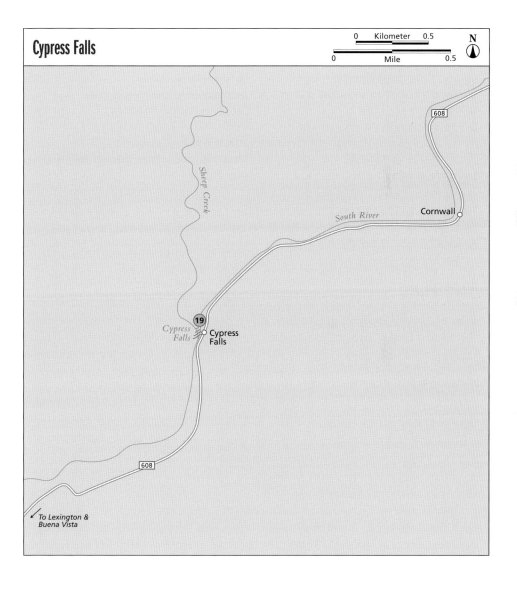

Cypress Falls

# 20 Lace Falls

The hike to the Natural Bridge is so short, why not keep going on to Lace Falls? After all, it's flat and easy and there are a number of kitschy-cool sights along the way.

**Height:** 35 feet in a series of slides
**Start:** I started my GPS unit after I paid the lady at the Natural Bridge Visitor Center and walked outside. So this hike is from the top of the many stairs immediately below you.
**Distance:** 2.2 miles out and back
**Difficulty:** Easy/moderate
**Canine compatibility:** No dogs allowed at Natural Bridge park (at least until this becomes part of the state park system)
**Trail surface:** Crushed gravel

**Hiking time:** About 1 hour
**Blaze color:** None
**County:** Rockbridge
**Land status:** Owned by the nonprofit Virginia Conservation Legacy Fund
**Trail contact:** Virginia Conservation Legacy Fund, (800) 533-1410; www.conservationlegacyfund.org; info@naturalbridgeva.com
**Maps:** *DeLorme, Virginia Atlas and Gazetteer:* page 53, C6

**Finding the trailhead:** From I-81 south of Lexington, get off on exit 180 and drive south on US 11 for just under 4 miles to Natural Bridge. Pull into the parking lot and enter the giant visitor center. **GPS:** N37 37.698' / W79 32.611'

## The Hike

I visited Natural Bridge Park and Lace Falls a few months after the news broke that the Natural Bridge itself and much of the surrounding property, including Lace Falls, would be sold to the state to create a state park. This is great news; we just don't know when it will happen. As a state park, there will be so much more for outdoors lovers to do here. Of course, this is terrible news if you come to places of natural wonder to buy stuffed animals and you prefer your trails wide, groomed, and walled off from the creeks they run alongside.

No matter when you come here, though, you probably aren't coming for Lace Falls.

That's totally understandable. The Natural Bridge itself truly is jaw-dropping in its size and scope. It seems totally incongruous for where it is located. It should be on every Virginian's state bucket list.

But it's also very close to the entrance to the park. Down some steps, around a corner, and there it is. Boom. And since you can only stare at something for so long, even something as cool as the Natural Bridge, why not keep walking to Lace Falls?

The only complaint I have about the falls—a series of slides—is that you can't get very close to them. Hopefully that will change when the park becomes a state park. In the meantime enjoy the flat hike and the random sights along the way, like the "Lost River" and the replica Monacan Indian village.

# Lace Falls

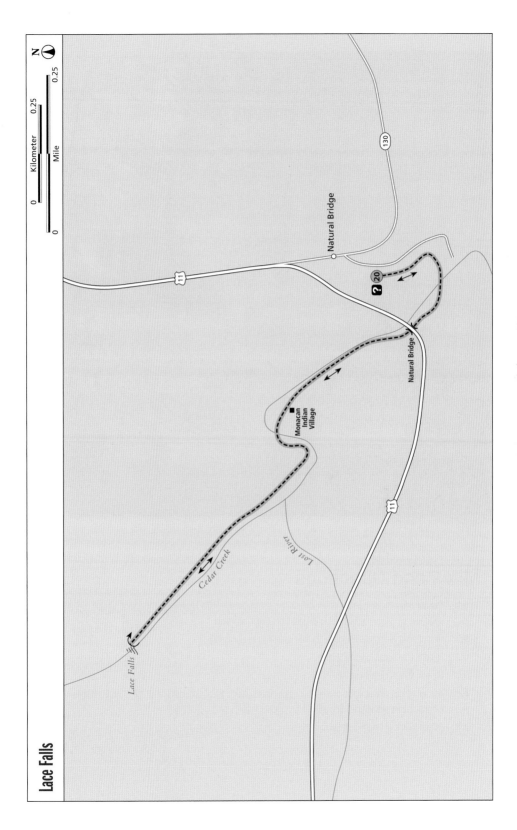

Kilometer
0        0.25

Mile
0        0.25

N

Natural Bridge

130

11

?  20

Natural Bridge

Monacan
Indian
Village

Cedar Creek

Lost River

Lace Falls

11

*This hike takes you to an observation area about 100 yards downstream of Lace Falls.*

## Miles and Directions

**0.0**  Pay at the visitor center. Walk down the stairs inside the building, then exit to the top of a long set of stairs outside. Let's call that the trailhead.

**0.2**  Reach the Natural Bridge. Gawk in slack-jawed wonder.

**0.5**  Reach the Monacan Village.

**0.7**  Reach the "Lost River."

**1.1**  Arrive at the observation area for Lace Falls (GPS: N37 38.053' / W79 33.251'), then retrace your steps to the trailhead.

**2.2**  Arrive back at the trailhead.

# FUTURE OF NATURAL BRIDGE

For years Natural Bridge (and Lace Falls upstream) was as much a tourist trap as it was a natural wonder. To be sure, the private park/resort boasted tremendous beauty, but it was marred, in my estimation, by the schlocky gift shop, the wax museum, and other such circus-like attractions that took away from the park's grandeur.

All that is set to change, however, because the natural bridge and the 1,500 surrounding acres once owned by Thomas Jefferson are set to become a Virginia State Park by the end of 2015. That agreement was announced in early 2014 and ended 240 years of private ownership that began with Jefferson, who purchased it from King George III.

The almost-200-foot-tall rock formation draws about 200,000 visitors a year and since 1988 has been owned by Washington, DC, developer Angelo Puglisi. He agreed to sell the property to the Virginia Conservation Legacy Fund, which will eventually deed the property to the state.

This is great news for lovers of waterfalls and natural wonders like the giant limestone arch that gives the local town its name. Who knows, by the time you read this—or get out to the James River Valley to see Lace Falls—the park may already be in state hands.

*You can't get to Lace Falls without going under the Natural Bridge, which, let's be honest, is really why you're here anyway.*

# Blue Ridge Parkway

The Blue Ridge Parkway waterfalls probably have the greatest variety of any section in this book. Crabtree Falls might be the most famous falls in Virginia. Saint Mary's Falls could be the hardest to get to. Apple Orchard is an underrated gem. Bent Mountain Falls has the second-highest sheer drop. Panther Falls is, for my money, Virginia's best waterfall–swimming hole combination (complete with perfect jumping rock).

So, needless to say, waterfall lovers will spend plenty of time on the Blue Ridge Parkway in their search for gorgeous falling water. But the Parkway itself is an impressive creation. Here are some fast facts about the famous strip of pavement:

- The Blue Ridge Parkway is 469 miles long and links Great Smoky Mountains National Park with Shenandoah National Park.

- The Parkway, while not technically a natural national park, has been the most visited unit in the National Park System every year since 1946, except 1949 and 2013. Over 15 million people drove some portion of the Parkway in 2012.

- The Parkway was started under the Franklin D. Roosevelt administration (1936) but was not completed until Ronald Reagan was president (1987).

- While the Parkway connects to Skyline Drive at Rockfish Gap, the two roads are managed by separate NPS units. Skyline Drive, at 105 miles long, is part of Shenandoah National Park.

- The Parkway will be depicted on North Carolina's version of the "America the Beautiful" quarter in 2015.

The Blue Ridge Parkway is also the quintessential fall foliage route (along with Skyline Drive) in Virginia. What a trip it would be to combine waterfall hunting with leaf peeping! Typically, the Parkway experiences the color change around mid-October, but many factors contribute to when and where colors peak. The Parkway varies in elevation from just under 650 feet where it crosses the James River to over 6,000 feet south of Mount Pisgah in North Carolina. The National Park Service makes regular fall foliage updates to its Blue Ridge Parkway website at nps.gov/blri. Just keep in mind that weather up on the Parkway can change drastically, even in the fall. If snows come in, chances are affected sections will be closed until they're passable.

# 21 St. Mary's Falls

Put your best hiking boots on for this one, and lace 'em up tight! Or better yet, if you go in the warm months, wear some shoes you don't mind getting wet. There's no other hike in this book like the one to St. Mary's Falls.

**Height:** 15 feet
**Start:** There's an obvious trailhead for the St. Mary's Trail at the east end of the parking area.
**Distance:** 4.6 miles out and back
**Difficulty:** Strenuous due to erratic trail conditions
**Canine compatibility:** There is no leash requirement in general areas of the George Washington National Forest, but there are some sections of this trail where a dog would be better off walking down the creek instead of trying to navigate.
**Trail surface:** Runs the gamut from hard-packed dirt to rocky, rooty singletrack to scree fields to the river itself
**Hiking time:** About 3 hours
**Blaze color:** None
**County:** Rockbridge
**Land status:** George Washington National Forest
**Trail contact:** (540) 265-5100; USDA Forest Service, (888) 265-0019; www.fs.usda .gov/gwj. Forest Supervisor's Office, 5162 Valleypointe Parkway, Roanoke 24019
**Maps:** DeLorme, Virginia Atlas and Gazetteer: page 54, A3

**Finding the trailhead:** From I-81 in Raphine, at exit 205, go east on CR 606 for 1.6 miles. Take a left and drive north on US 11 for 0.1 mile. Then take a right on SR 56 (Tye River Gap Road) and drive 1.1 miles to CR 608. Go left on CR 608 and drive 2.1 miles. At that point you'll cross a creek and you'll have to turn right to stay on CR 608. Do that, then drive 0.2 mile and turn right on FR 41 (St. Mary's Road). Take the gravel FR 41 just over a mile to where it dead-ends at a parking area. **GPS:** N37 55.501' / W79 08.221'

## The Hike

Where to begin with the hike to Saint Mary's Falls? First, there is no other hike remotely like it in this book. That's because it's in the St. Mary's Wilderness area of the George Washington National Forest. And unlike regular-use areas of the national forest, wilderness areas have very little in the way of signage or maintained trails. Oh, there are trails, of course, but if a tree falls across one, it's not getting chainsawed and moved away anytime soon. Wilderness areas are meant to be just that. The only sign visible on the trail when I hiked it was the one at the 1.2-mile mark saying which way the St. Mary's Trail went. It was old and leaning against a tree, and it could very well be somewhere else by the time you read this.

More than anything, know this before you hike to the falls: You're in for an adventure. You will almost certainly lose the trail at some point or you'll swear it no longer exists. It starts off like a normal trail, but at the fork near the 1-mile mark, you have to cross the creek for the first time, and everything changes. Some sections

*You'll have earned a meal and a long rest by the time you reach St. Mary's Falls. Bring some stout boots for this one.*

that hug the steep riverside cliffs have clearly been washed away by storms. Others look like they could fall into the creek at any moment. You'll cross scree fields where the footing is poor at best. And the river level will completely determine where you can cross and where you can't. After a big storm you probably shouldn't attempt this at all.

But here's the main thing to remember: If you're determined to see St. Mary's Falls—and you should be because it is a stunning falls in a serene, secluded setting—just stay with the river. The trail may appear and disappear. It may be brutal on the ankles and even hazardous at times, but if you hug the river and persevere, you'll reach the falls.

One of the keys to doing that is footwear. If it's a hot summer day, some river shoes with a good thick sole wouldn't be the worst idea. They would allow you to just hop in the creek and cross it instead of waiting for the perfect rock-hopping spot. But if it's too cold for that, sturdy hiking shoes are the next best option. This is a rock-scrambling adventure, and regular sneakers won't cut it. Better yet: Do this hike with someone who already has. It'll eliminate all the guesswork about where the trail is and where to cross the stream.

# St. Mary's Falls

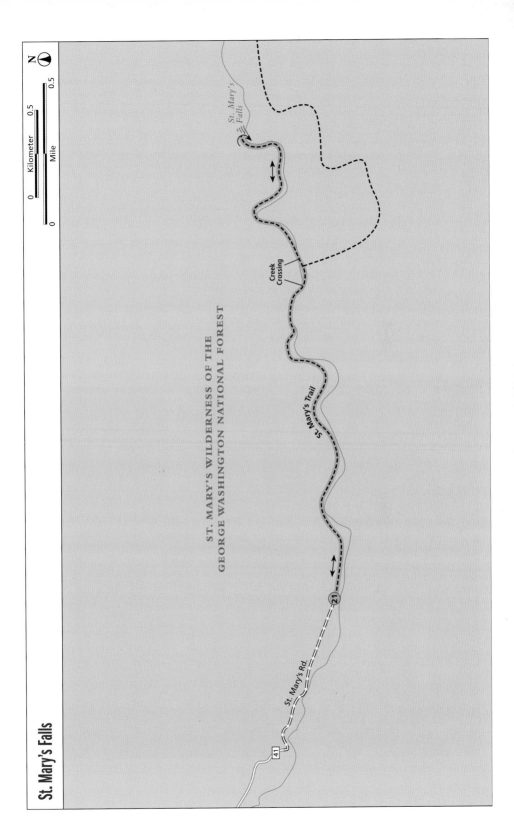

St. Mary's Falls

Creek Crossing

St. Mary's Trail

St. Mary's Rd.

41

21

ST. MARY'S WILDERNESS OF THE
GEORGE WASHINGTON NATIONAL FOREST

N

0          Kilometer          0.5

0                                0.5
Mile

The falls itself isn't terribly high, but it's in a gorgeous mountain valley, and after the effort you put in to reach it, you'll swear it's the best waterfall you've ever laid eyes on.

## Miles and Directions

**0.0** Start at the trailhead and hike east on the St. Mary's Trail along the St. Mary's River.

**1.0** At a fork in the trail, follow the right fork toward the river, rock-hop across the river, and pick up the trail on the other side.

**1.2** The St. Mary's Trail goes off to the right. Stay left (really more straight than left) on the unnamed trail that parallels the river.

**1.3** Cross back over to the left side of the river (when looking upstream) and find the trail right along the riverbank.

**1.6** You'll see a beautiful overhanging rock and the river cutting a narrow path below it. The river corridor begins to feel more like a canyon here.

**2.0** Cross back over to the right side of the river (when looking upstream) for the final time.

**2.2** Arrive at the falls (GPS: N37 55.781' / W79 06.435'), then retrace your steps (good luck!).

**4.6** Arrive back at the trailhead.

*It's not easy to stay on the trail on this wilderness hike. Stay with the St. Mary's River and you'll find the falls.*

# SAINT MARY'S WILDERNESS

In 1964 Congress passed and President Lyndon Johnson signed into law the Wilderness Act—with the swipe of a pen officially protecting 9.1 million acres of federal land.

The act was succinct: *A wilderness, in contrast with those areas where man and his own works dominate the landscape, is hereby recognized as an area where the earth and its community of life are untrammeled by man, where man himself is a visitor who does not remain.*

Twenty years later the 9,835-acre Saint Mary's Wilderness in George Washington National Forest became part of the system. It's the largest designated wilderness in Virginia and the only one that has a hike featured in this book. The wilderness ranges in elevation from 1,700 feet (where your waterfall hike begins) to 3,640 feet and includes the upper portion of the Saint Mary's River watershed, including the Cellar Hollow and Spy Run drainages. The area was mined for iron ore and manganese until the 1950s, and evidence of those activities remains along the Saint Mary's River gorge.

If the hike to Saint Mary's seems different than any other hike in this book, that's probably because of the wilderness designation. Wilderness areas aren't managed like other public lands. When trees fall across the trail, they tend to stay there for a long time.

When a trail gets washed out by a flood, hikers have to find another way to their destination. Frankly, that's the allure of a place like the Saint Mary's Wilderness and the hike to Saint Mary's Falls. The trail isn't manicured. Signage is minimal. You're in the middle of nowhere. It's good to know those kinds of places still exist, isn't it?

# 22 White Rock Falls

A short hike, an unexpected overlook, a rock scramble, and a lovely woodland waterfall . . . what's not to like at White Rock Falls?

**Height:** A drop of about 25 feet
**Start:** Park at the Slacks Overlook, but the hike actually starts at the trailhead back across and a few yards north on the Blue Ridge Parkway.
**Distance:** 1.2 miles out and back
**Difficulty:** Moderate
**Canine compatibility:** Dogs must be on a 6-foot leash.
**Trail surface:** Narrow but not particularly rocky

**Hiking time:** 45 minutes to 1 hour
**Blaze color:** Red
**County:** Nelson
**Land status:** National Park
**Trail contact:** Blue Ridge Parkway. nps.gov/blri/; Park headquarters: 199 Hemphill Knob Road, Asheville, NC 28803
**Maps:** *DeLorme, Virginia Atlas and Gazetteer:* page 54, A3

**Finding the trailhead:** Park at the Slacks Overlook parking area on the west side of the Blue Ridge Parkway between mileposts 19 and 20. Walk north from the parking area, cross the Blue Ridge Parkway, and you'll see the trailhead where it enters the woods just a few yards down the road. **GPS:** N37 54.420' / W79 03.090'

## The Hike

This is one of the longer hikes in the Blue Ridge Parkway region, though at 1.2 miles it isn't terribly long. And it offers the added bonus of a rock outcrop with great views of distant mountains.

The hike itself is pretty straightforward until you reach the outcrop (with views of the Priest). One source I used said to follow the trail past the outcrop to a switchback that would bring me back under the outcrop and to the base of White Rock Falls. I never found that switchback, so I did what I'm recommending here, which actually shortens the hike a bit.

At the rock outcrop look down and you'll see that you can scramble down between two giant boulders. It's steep, and the dirt is a bit loose, but it's doable. Once down below the rocks, head left on the trail for maybe a couple hundred feet to reach the falls.

White Rock Falls has an almost delicate feel to it. In summer if it hasn't rained, there won't be a ton of water in it. And it feels like it's falling right out of the forest. This one doesn't have the notoriety of some nearby falls—like Crabtree and Saint Mary's—but it's well worth the effort if you're up on the Parkway.

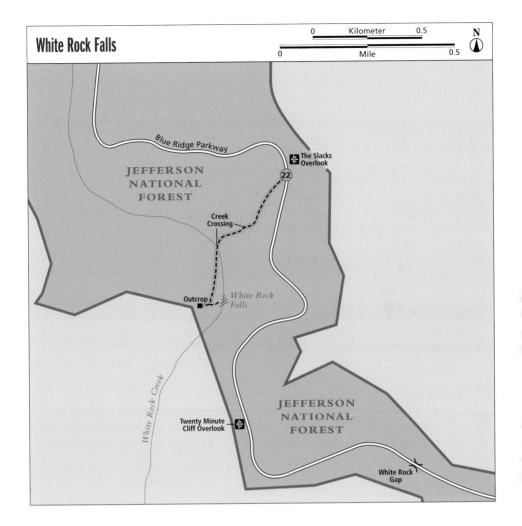

**White Rock Falls**

## Miles and Directions

**0.0**  Start at the Slacks Overlook.

**0.1**  Cross the Parkway, walk north, and find the trailhead where the trail enters the woods. You can't miss it.

**0.3**  Cross the creek.

**0.4**  Cross the creek again.

**0.5**  Reach a rock outcrop with great mountain views.

**0.6**  Arrive at the base of the falls (GPS: N37 54.142' / W79 03.277'), then retrace your steps.

**1.2**  Arrive back at the trailhead.

# 23 Crabtree Falls

Crabtree Falls may or may not be the highest falls east of the Mississippi, but it's definitely the most famous waterfall in Virginia. Here's a place where the hikers' hype is well earned.

**Height:** Over 1,000 feet in many drops
**Start:** The trailhead and facilities are at the far end of the parking lot from where you enter.
**Distance:** 3.4 miles out and back
**Difficulty:** Strenuous
**Canine compatibility:** There is no leash requirement in general areas of the George Washington National Forest.
**Trail surface:** Rooty, rocky singletrack
**Hiking time:** About 2 hours

**Blaze color:** None
**County:** Amherst
**Land status:** George Washington National Forest
**Trail contact:** USDA Forest Service, (888) 265-0019; www.fs.usda.gov/gwj; Forest Supervisor's Office, 5162 Valleypointe Parkway, Roanoke 24019
**Maps:** DeLorme, Virginia Atlas and Gazetteer: page 54, B3

**Finding the trailhead:** From the Blue Ridge Parkway between mileposts 27 and 28 (Tye River Gap), drive east on SR 56 for almost 7 miles to the parking area on the right. **GPS:** N37 51.054' / W79 04.744'

## The Hike

Should you ever take on the challenge of writing a book about hiking to waterfalls in Virginia, the first question many people will ask you is, "Have you done Crabtree Falls yet?" And once you've hiked it, you'll realize why it's famous. Hiking Crabtree Falls is one of those experiences that lives up to its considerable reputation.

First, the hike is not easy. You'll climb just under 1,100 feet in 1.7 miles, constantly switching back. But every so often, just when you'll feel like you've earned one, you'll come to an observation area or a break in the foliage where you can take in some more of the falls or the mountains in the distance.

When I went in late May, purple rhododendrons were blooming all along the hike, some hanging out over Crabtree Creek as it fell from one pool to the next. It was absolutely stunning. The only disappointing thing about Crabtree Falls is that there's no one place to take it all in. Even in winter, you can't see it all. When you reach the top and cross the creek on the wooden bridge, you'll have a great view of the Blue Ridge Mountains in the distance but not a good one of the falls. Whatever you do, don't try to get too close in search of that elusive view. Signs all over the area warn that twenty-three people have died at the falls over the years from not realizing how slippery the rocks can be and falling great distances.

Still, even without that one view of it all, Crabtree is a Virginia hiking experience not to be missed. Just be sure to bring food and drink so you can refuel at the top. You'll need it.

*Go at the right time in May, and your hike to the top of Crabtree Falls will include these beautiful rhododendron blooms.*

*It's almost as hard to count the number of sections there are in Crabtree Falls as it is to photograph them all at once.*

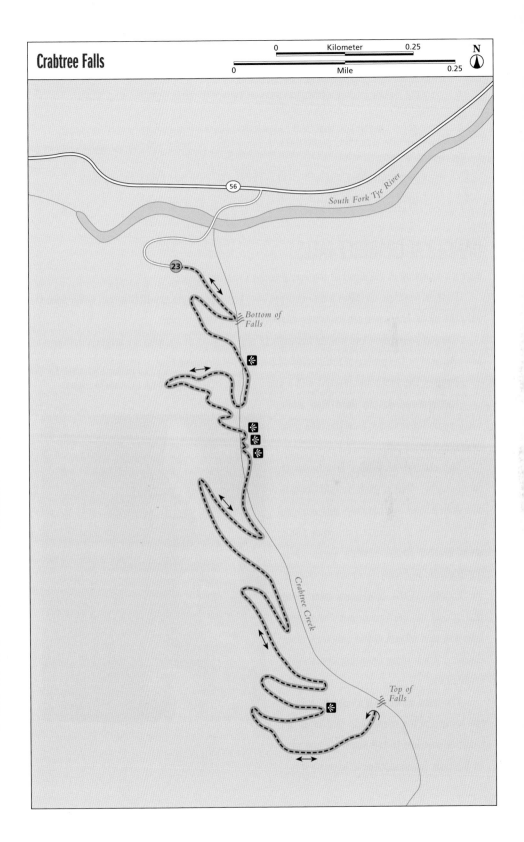

# Miles and Directions

**0.0** From the parking lot, begin hiking on a paved surface to the observation area for the lowest falls.

**0.2** Arrive at the observation area for the lowest falls. There are many observation areas and places to take in the falls over the next 1.5 miles, but the trail is well marked. There's no way to get lost.

**1.7** Arrive at the top of the falls (GPS: N37 50.632' / W79 04.507'). Retrace your steps.

**3.4** Arrive back at the trailhead.

# DANGER AT CRABTREE FALLS

Here's a sampling of the signs at the very popular Crabtree Falls:

Danger! Multiple fatalities have occurred here because people got off this trail and climbed onto the rocks. The rocks are extremely slippery due to a clear algae.

Danger! Young men and women between 18 and 25 years of age who are bright, intelligent, and educated fit the profile of the victims of the siren of Crabtree Falls.

Danger! The rocks are covered with a plant growth that makes them extremely slippery.

Twenty-three people have died while climbing on these rocks. View the falls from designated areas only.

The number of deaths is now up to twenty-eight. That's twenty-eight people who didn't heed the warnings and plunged to their deaths at Crabtree Falls since 1982, when the US Forest Service began keeping records. Not only is Crabtree dangerous because of the sometimes-clear algae that grows on the rocks, but the remote area and lack of cell phone coverage make rescue a much more daunting and lengthy proposition.

The good news is it's easy to take in the beauty of the many falls that make up Crabtree and live to tell about it: Just stay on the trail. It sounds simple because it is.

*Be careful at the big and beautiful but dangerous Crabtree Falls. Twenty-eight people have died there since 1982.*

# 24 Wigwam Falls

Wigwam Falls is a lovely woodland cascade that, despite its easy accessibility, is less well known than others along this stretch of the Blue Ridge Parkway. And you get a bonus history lesson from the signage near the falls.

**Height:** A sliding cascade of about 25 feet
**Start:** The trailhead is obvious once you enter the Yankee Horse Ridge parking area.
**Distance:** 250 feet out and back
**Difficulty:** Easy
**Canine compatibility:** Dogs must be leashed in all areas of the Blue Ridge Parkway.
**Trail surface:** Roots, hard-packed dirt
**Hiking time:** 5–10 minutes

**Blaze color:** None
**County:** Nelson
**Land status:** National Park
**Trail contact:** Blue Ridge Parkway, nps.gov/blri/; park headquarters: 199 Hemphill Knob Road, Asheville, NC 28803
**Maps:** *DeLorme, Virginia Atlas and Gazetteer:* page 54, B2

**Finding the trailhead:** The Yankee Horse Ridge parking area is on the east side of the Blue Ridge Parkway between mileposts 34 and 35. **GPS:** N37 48.561' / W79 10.788'

## The Hike

The hike is short but highlighted by an old narrow-gauge railroad bed—the Irish Creek Railway—used for logging decades ago. When it was completed in 1920, it was 50 miles long and helped haul the trees off the mountain and down into the valley below.

Technically this falls is on a branch that feeds nearby Wigwam Creek, but I guess it was close enough for naming purposes. No matter what you call it, what you've got here is your quintessential woodland waterfall. The feeling is intimate at Wigwam Falls. It's the kind of cascade that you don't hear from very far off because the volume of water isn't great. But the way the stream slides down the surface of the granite, while moss and ferns grow thick on the forest floor below, imparts a serenity to this place. It's a great spot to stop and stretch the legs if you're driving the Blue Ridge Parkway and have been in the car a while.

*The Wigwam Falls hike is short and easy with a history lesson thrown in.*

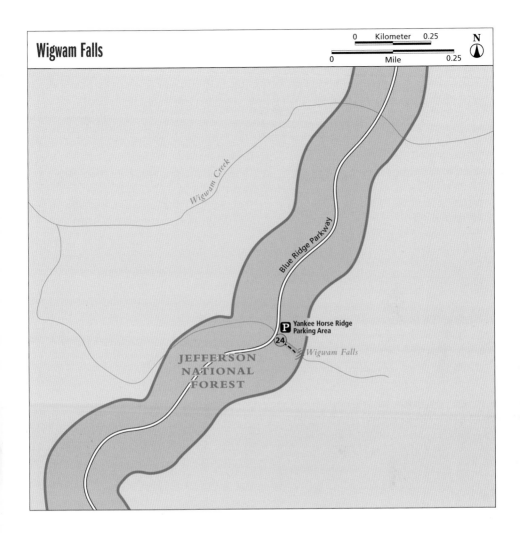

## Miles and Directions

**0.0** From the parking lot, follow the obvious trail at the trailhead.

**0.025** Arrive at the falls (GPS: N37 48.526' / W79 10.756').

**0.05** Arrive back at the trailhead.

# 25 Statons Creek Falls

Most people just observe the upper section of Statons Creek Falls from beside the road, but a short, steep bushwhack rewards the intrepid waterfall hound with an impressively tall falls.

**Height:** About 125 feet over multiple drops
**Start:** There's a small parking area across CR 633 from the top of the falls.
**Distance:** Roadside
**Difficulty:** Easy
**Canine compatibility:** N/A
**Trail surface:** N/A
**Hiking time:** N/A
**Blaze color:** N/A

**County:** Amherst
**Land status:** George Washington National Forest
**Trail contact:** USDA Forest Service, (888) 265-0019; www.fs.usda.gov/gwj. Forest Supervisor's Office, 5162 Valleypointe Parkway, Roanoke 24019
**Maps:** *DeLorme, Virginia Atlas and Gazetteer:* page 54, B2

**Finding the trailhead:** From the junction of the Blue Ridge Parkway and US 60, head east on US 60 3.3 miles and turn left on CR 605 (Pedlar River Road). Drive 1.7 miles and stay right at a fork onto CR 633 (Fiddlers Green Way, which is gravel). It's just over 1 mile to an obvious pullout on the right across the road from the top of the falls. **GPS:** N37 46.101' / W79 14.152'

*This picture shows maybe the top 25 percent of Statons Creek Falls. Be very careful up here. The rocks can be deceivingly slick.*

# The Hike

From the road, when the leaves are on the trees, you get only a tantalizing glimpse of the powerful Statons Creek Falls. Even in winter you can't see it all from the road. And where you park is across the road from the very top of the falls—you can see maybe 30 percent of the falls from up there—so that angle is unsatisfying too.

The only solution is to bushwhack down to the base of the falls. The way is steep but not really dangerous. Follow the sound of water falling over 125 feet of granite in multiple sections—three main ones—and you eventually arrive at a very impressive waterfall. Because it takes a bit of work to get there, Statons is one of those rare waterfalls that is striking and not usually very crowded.

**Note:** Be very careful if you choose to scamper down the upper portion of the falls from the road. It can be done safely, but a fall up here would invite serious injury.

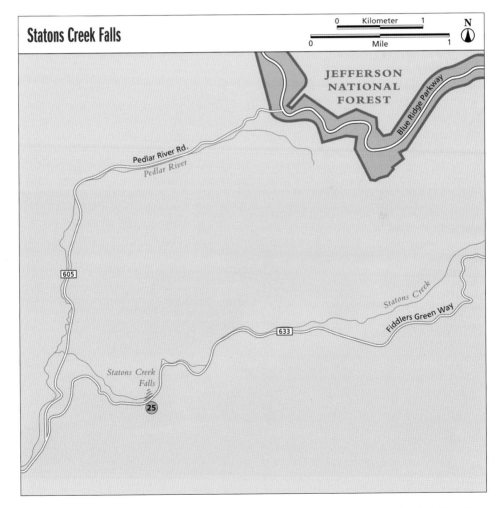

# 26 Panther Falls

Panther Falls is the quintessential waterfall–swimming hole combination. When the weather is nice, this is one popular place—and for good reason. Not only are the multiple swimming holes beautiful, they're deep enough to safely jump off the overhanging boulders.

**Height:** 15 feet in 2 distinct drops
**Start:** The trailhead, with signage and kiosk, starts at the gravel parking area on the left of Panther Falls Road (which fills up quickly in the summer).
**Distance:** 650 yards out and back
**Difficulty:** Easy
**Canine compatibility:** There is no leash requirement in general areas of the George Washington National Forest.
**Trail surface:** Rooty, hard-packed dirt

**Hiking time:** 5–10 minutes
**Blaze color:** None
**County:** Amherst
**Land status:** George Washington National Forest
**Trail contact:** USDA Forest Service, (888) 265-0019; www.fs.usda.gov/gwj. Forest Supervisor's Office, 5162 Valleypointe Parkway, Roanoke 24019
**Maps:** *DeLorme, Virginia Atlas and Gazetteer:* page 54, C1

**Finding the trailhead:** From the Blue Ridge Parkway between milepost 45 and 46, just east of the town of Buena Vista, go east on US 60 for 0.1 mile and turn right onto FR 315 (Panther Falls Road). Follow this gravel road just over 3 miles to an obvious parking area with a trailhead on the left. **GPS:** N37 43.203' / W79 17.499'

*Popular Panther Falls offers the quintessential waterfall/swimming hole experience.*

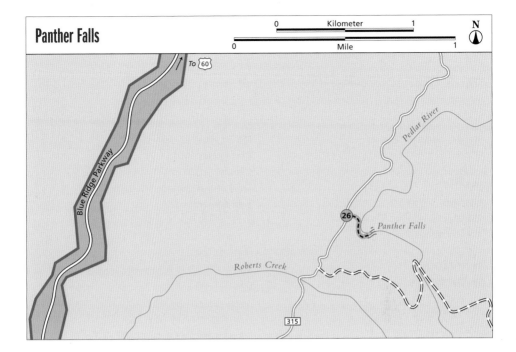

## The Hike

If you like solitude, this may not be the falls for you (except in winter). Then again, if you want a great place to let the kids splash around and jump off huge rocks into deep pools in a gorgeous mountain setting (with dozens of your closest friends), Panther Falls on the Pedlar River should be near the top of your list.

While the falls itself—two distinct drops of about 15 to 20 feet total—won't wow you, the ease of getting here and the swimming, jumping, picnicking, and general carousing options you'll find once you arrive at the falls are regionally famous. That's why you won't be alone unless it's dawn or the dead of winter.

As for the hike itself, there's not much to it: Follow the trail from the gravel parking lot down to the top of the falls. Set up shop on the nearest patch of rock and hop in.

## Miles and Directions

**0.0** Start at the obvious trail at the trailhead.

**0.2** Arrive at the top of the falls (GPS: N37 43.134' / W79 17.408').

**0.4** Arrive back at the trailhead.

# 27 Apple Orchard Falls

This is one of my top five surprises in this book and a personal favorite hike. Seek this one out if you're driving on the Blue Ridge Parkway in Virginia.

**Height:** About 85 feet
**Start:** You can't miss the trailhead here at the Sunset Field Overlook. It's right there in Sunset Field.
**Distance:** 2.7 miles out and back
**Difficulty:** Moderate/strenuous
**Canine compatibility:** There is no leash requirement in general areas of the Jefferson National Forest.
**Trail surface:** Rocky singletrack, steep at the end

**Hiking time:** 1-2 hours
**Blaze color:** White
**County:** Botetourt
**Land status:** Jefferson National Forest
**Trail contact:** USDA Forest Service, (888) 265-0019; www.fs.usda.gov/gwj. Forest Supervisor's Office, 5162 Valleypointe Parkway, Roanoke 24019
**Maps:** *DeLorme, Virginia Atlas and Gazetteer:* page 53, D6

**Finding the trailhead:** Park at the Sunset Field Overlook on the west side of the Blue Ridge Parkway between mileposts 78 and 79. **GPS:** N37 30.472' / W79 31.447'

## The Hike

Maybe it's my own fault that the awesomeness (and I don't use that word lightly) of this waterfall-hike combo came as a surprise. I don't know why I didn't really have high expectations when I started this hike, but I didn't. It's not that they were low—they just weren't high.

Then I started hiking, and I knew I was in for a treat. It was a beautiful late-May day with no humidity and no one else around. Like all Blue Ridge Parkway–area trails, this one was well marked. I passed a couple of trail junctions in the first 0.7 mile and simply followed the signs for Apple Orchard Falls Trail.

Just before the 1-mile mark, you cross a wooden bridge, and if you look upstream, you'll find your first surprise: a drop of about 8 to 10 feet over a mossy boulder in the quiet of the woods. From here you'll also have a nice view of the mountains in the distance.

As you get closer to the falls, the trail will steepen dramatically—that's why I rated it moderate/strenuous—but it's not particularly difficult, technically, just steep. You're descending out of the view of the creek, then you turn back toward it and enter a tunnel of rhododendrons. After 30 feet or so, you exit right at the base of this 85-foot cataract. It just smacks you in the face with its height and power, and if, like me, you aren't expecting it, you'll be doubly blown away. There's some impressive bridge/deck work that was constructed years ago at the base of the falls, so take advantage of it and sit for a while.

You won't want to leave Apple Orchard Falls.

*Pair this hike with nearby Fallingwater Cascades for a Blue Ridge Parkway two-fer.*

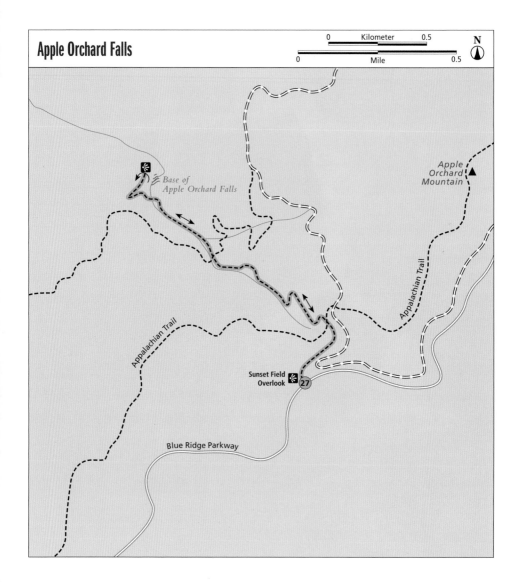

Apple Orchard Falls

0    Kilometer    0.5
0       Mile        0.5

N

Base of
Apple Orchard Falls

Apple
Orchard
Mountain

Appalachian Trail

Appalachian Trail

Sunset Field
Overlook    27

Blue Ridge Parkway

## Miles and Directions

**0.0**    Find the trailhead at the parking lot. Descend on Apple Orchard Falls Trail.

**0.2**    Reach the first trail junction, a four-way junction. Stay straight on Apple Orchard Falls Trail.

**0.5**    The creek comes up out of the ground on your left.

**0.7**    At the second trail junction, follow signs to stay on Apple Orchard Falls Trail.

**0.1**    Cross a wooden bridge over the creek. Look upstream for a beautiful 8-foot woodland falls.

**1.4**    Arrive at the base of the falls (GPS: N37 30.990' / W79 31.968') and retrace your steps to the trailhead.

**2.7**    Arrive back at the trailhead.

## WHENCE THE NAME APPLE ORCHARD FALLS?

Apple Orchard Creek doesn't fall over rock here creating Apple Orchard Falls. In fact, there is no Apple Orchard Creek in the area. So, where did the name for this waterfall come from? It came from the mountain you can see from the falls, Apple Orchard Mountain, and this mountain got its name due to a combination of weather and biology.

The slopes of the 4,225-foot mountain are covered with red oak, but the weather can be so severe in the winter that the oaks are stunted, looking as if they've been pruned. From a distance, it gives the appearance of an apple orchard.

# 28 Fallingwater Cascades

This falls is modest, but the hike isn't terribly long, and there's a nice mountain view along the way. A great Blue Ridge Parkway leg-stretcher.

**Height:** Over 30 feet in a series of cascades
**Start:** The trailhead is at the south end of the parking area.
**Distance:** 1.0 mile out and back
**Difficulty:** Easy/moderate
**Canine compatibility:** There is no leash requirement in general areas of the Jefferson National Forest.
**Trail surface:** Rocky singletrack
**Hiking time:** About 45 minutes

**Blaze color:** None
**County:** Botetourt
**Land status:** Jefferson National Forest
**Trail contact:** USDA Forest Service, (888) 265-0019; www.fs.usda.gov/gwj. Forest Supervisor's Office, 5162 Valleypointe Parkway, Roanoke, Virginia 24019
**Maps:** *DeLorme, Virginia Atlas and Gazetteer:* page 43, A6

**Finding the trailhead:** North of Peaks of Otter, the Fallingwater Cascades Parking Area is on the west side of the Blue Ridge Parkway between mileposts 83 and 84. **GPS:** N37 28.384' / W79 34.848'

*Fallingwater Cascades is not far from the popular Peaks of Otter section of the Parkway.*

# The Hike

This hike can be crowded because it's close to the Peaks of Otter area, and it's not terribly challenging. Still, it's worth pairing with nearby, and more impressive, Apple Orchard Falls if you're specifically seeking out Blue Ridge Parkway waterfalls or you just want to get out and get some exercise.

Like most hikes along the Blue Ridge Parkway, this one is well marked. A third of a mile into it, you'll cross a wooden bridge over Fallingwater Creek where you'll find lovely mountain views. The falls itself is actually a series of cascades. From the base, you can see the final 30 feet, and the forest hangs above this lower portion, adding an intimate feel.

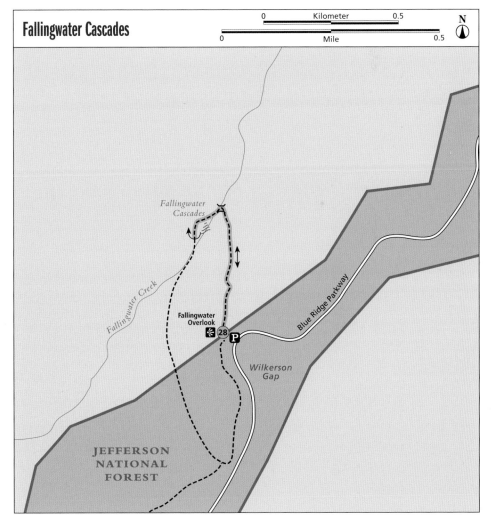

Fallingwater Cascades

# Miles and Directions

**0.0** Start at the south end of the parking area and follow the signs that point you to the falls.

**0.3** Cross a wooden bridge that offers nice mountain views.

**0.4** Go left at the trail junction to reach the base of the falls. Less than a half mile later, you'll reach the base of the falls (GPS: N37 28.583' / W79 34.902'). Retrace your steps to the trailhead.

**1.0** Arrive back at the trailhead.

# 29 Bent Mountain Falls

This is generally agreed to be Virginia's second-highest waterfall after Crabtree Falls, farther north along the Blue Ridge Parkway. And while Crabtree as a whole is certainly longer, it's possible Bent Mountain Falls has the longest single drop.

**Height:** 200 feet

**Start:** The hike starts where the gravel road dead ends at the gated entrance to Bottom Creek Gorge Preserve. Walk past the gate and follow the fire road.

**Distance:** 3.2 miles out and back

**Difficulty:** Easy/moderate

**Canine compatibility:** Dogs are not allowed on any Nature Conservancy property.

**Trail surface:** Hard-packed dirt singletrack

**Hiking time:** 1–2 hours

**Blaze color:** None at first, then red-blazed Johnston Trail

**County:** Montgomery

**Land status:** Nature Conservancy property

**Trail contact:** Nature Conservancy; nature.org (search "Bent Mountain Falls")

**Maps:** *DeLorme, Virginia Atlas and Gazetteer:* page 42, D1

**Finding the trailhead:** From I-81 in Roanoke, take exit 141 and drive south on SR 419 8.5 miles to US 221. Turn right on US 221 and drive 15 miles, then turn right on CR 644. Go just over 1 mile and bear right at a fork onto CR 669. After 1.5 miles you come to a T junction. Stay right on CR 669 and drive another 1 mile to a bridge over a creek. Just after the bridge, turn left on a gravel road, where you'll see Nature Conservancy signs. The parking area is 200 feet up the road at the gate. **GPS:** N37 07.987' / W80 10.973'

## The Hike

This waterfall hike is unlike any other in this book in that you're not actually hiking to the falls. You're hiking to an observation area where you can see the falls across a deep gorge—Bottom Creek Gorge. If you didn't know this going in, you'd probably be surprised, like I was. You hike enough waterfalls and you just expect certain things, like that sense you get of getting closer and closer to the falls, hearing it, etc.

But just because you don't end up very close to Bent Mountain Falls doesn't mean this isn't a worthy hike. Any excuse you can find to spend time on a Nature Conservancy property, you should take it. Bottom Creek Gorge Preserve is no exception. In addition, the falls itself may be far away, but it is very, very tall—200 feet by some estimates. I wouldn't be surprised if it were even higher. That makes it the second-highest falls in the state after Crabtree.

As for the hike itself, you start off on a fire road and hike 0.46 mile to the actual trail kiosk where there's a map and information on the preserve. Like most Nature Conservancy properties, the trails are very well marked here. After the informational kiosk, at the 0.83-mile mark, you'll stay left on the Johnston Trail. That's the most direct route to the observation area.

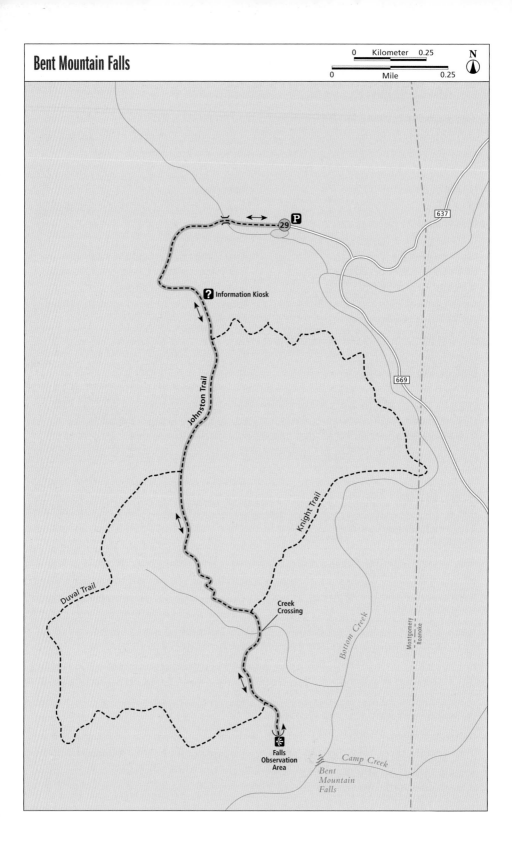

# Bent Mountain Falls

*This waterfall could boast the largest single drop of any Virginia cascade.*

Eventually the trail becomes more rocky and starts to trend downhill, but I don't think it rises to the level of even a moderate-difficulty hike. This one is definitely family friendly, but just don't get your hopes up about basking in the cooling mists of a giant waterfall. Bent Mountain Falls is for your eyes only.

## Miles and Directions

**0.0**   Begin the hike at the gated entrance to Bottom Creek Gorge Preserve on a fire road.

**0.1**   Cross a small bridge over a tiny creek.

**0.5**   Arrive at the trail kiosk, where you'll find information on the preserve and pamphlets. Eight-tenths of a mile later, you'll reach the junction with the yellow-blazed Knight Trail. Do not take that. Stay on your current trail, the red-blazed Johnston Trail.

**0.8**   At the junction with the Duval Trail, stay left on the Johnston Trail.

**0.9**   Notice the distinct change to a more open hardwood forest.

**1.2**   Knight Trail rejoins the Johnston Trail.

**1.3**   Blue-blazed Duval Trail rejoins the Johnston Trail.

**1.5**   Arrive at the observation area for the falls (GPS: N37 07.066' / W80 10.984'), then retrace your steps to the trailhead.

**3.2**   Arrive back at the trailhead.

# BOTTOM CREEK GORGE PRESERVE

The Nature Conservancy protects two areas near Roanoke that contain very different kinds of waterfalls. The Waterfall at Falls Ridge, located in the Falls Ridge Preserve, is featured in the Valley and Ridge section of this book. Bent Mountain Falls, by contrast, is up in the Blue Ridge Mountains in the much larger Bottom Creek Gorge Preserve.

Bottom Creek Gorge would be a worthy hiking and exploring destination even without Virginia's second-highest waterfall to recommend it. According to the Nature Conservancy, Bottom Creek Gorge is a hotbed for rare aquatic species, containing three rare fish and one globally rare plant. The creek is critical habitat for four species of fish native to the headwaters of the Roanoke River: the orangefin madtom, the bigeye jumprock, the riverweed darter, and the Roanoke darter. It also contains approximately 10 percent of all fish species known to be from Virginia, including native brook trout.

A half-acre shale barren provides habitat for the globally rare chestnut lipfern. Formerly known only from north-central Mexico to the southwestern United States, this lipfern occurs in isolated patches in southwestern Virginia and eastern West Virginia.

And an old-growth hemlock forest rising from the north side of the creek remained largely untouched due to its inaccessibility. A mix of forest and field covers the rest of the preserve. Mixed hardwood stands of tulip poplar, maple, oak, and hickory are complemented by several meadows and dense rhododendron thickets in ravines.

So, while Bent Mountain Falls draws most of the attention at Bottom Creek Gorge Preserve, the rare plants and fish species in this beautiful and dramatic mountain setting make the area a true Virginia gem.

# Shenandoah National Park

Shenandoah National Park could just be waterfall heaven. There are so many dramatic waterfalls in the park that it changed my sense of perspective and thus what I defined as a waterfall for this book. For every SNP entry here, there's at least one I left out, falls that would have qualified if they were sitting in the Piedmont or up in northern Virginia. But that's the nature of a book like this. I didn't want to send you to a so-so falls (by Shenandoah standards) if a whopper lay just down Skyline Drive. Reader-author trust is everything in a book like this, and I hope you'll agree that these are the best of what Shenandoah National Park has to offer.

Speaking of the park itself, about 1.2 million people visit Shenandoah every year, and when your waterfall quest brings you here, you should consider making a multiday trip of it. The park offers a huge variety of experiences and amenities. You can tent-camp in the backcountry (with a permit) or at organized sites like Lewis Mountain (milepost 57.5), Mathews Arm (milepost 22.1), Big Meadows (milepost 51.2), or Loft Mountain (milepost 79.5). Mathews Arm, Big Meadows, and Loft Mountain campgrounds also have pull-through and deep back-in sites, most of which are large enough to handle an RV with a tow vehicle. There's also formal lodging at Big Meadows, Skyland Resort, and cabins at Lewis Mountain.

The Shenandoah National Park visitor centers offer a wealth of park information, including how to join a ranger-guided hike and what kid-friendly options may be available. The Dickey Ridge Visitor Center lies at milepost 4.6 on Skyline Drive, and the Harry F. Byrd Sr. Visitor Center sits across from Big Meadows at milepost 51. The best place to start your Shenandoah National Park adventure (aside from this book, of course) is probably the park's website, nps.gov/shen.

The park is divided into three ranger districts—North, Central, and South—thus the divisions in this book. The North District stretches from Front Royal at the park's northern boundary south to Thornton Gap where US 211 comes up from Sperryville and Luray. The Central District is Shenandoah's largest in land area, running 34 miles from Thornton Gap to US 33, which connects Elkton on the west side of the park to Stanardsville on the east. The South District is the longest. Skyline Drive winds 40 miles through the South District to the park's boundary at Afton Mountain and Rockfish Gap.

# 30 Lands Run Falls

This is a good warm-up hike to an intimate woodland waterfall if you're entering Shenandoah National Park from the north.

**Height:** About 65 feet in 3 separate drops
**Start:** Don't take the singletrack trail west from the parking lot. Start at the lot's south end southbound on the yellow-blazed fire road.
**Distance:** 1.1–1.4 miles out and back, depending on amount of additional exploring
**Difficulty:** Moderate
**Canine compatibility:** Dogs must be on a 6-foot leash in Shenandoah National Park.
**Trail surface:** Gravel fire road, then an off-trail scramble to see the falls

**Hiking time:** About 45 minutes
**Blaze color:** Yellow
**County:** Warren
**Land status:** National Park
**Trail contact:** Shenandoah National Park: (540) 999-3500; nps.gov/shen. 3655 Highway 211 East, Luray 22835
**Maps:** DeLorme, Virginia Atlas and Gazetteer: page 74, B3

**Finding the trailhead:** The parking lot had no signage when I visited, but it's the only gravel lot on the west side of Skyline Drive between mileposts 9 and 10. **GPS:** N38 50.034' / W78 11.146'

## The Hike

This one is pretty simple until you reach the actual falls. Just hike a little over a half mile to the top of the falls. You won't even see tiny Lands Run until you're there, and you'll know you're there when you see two corrugated metal pipes that take the creek under the trail almost right to the top of the falls on the right.

From there you'll have to scramble down a pretty steep bank on either side of the falls.

The main drawback of Lands Run Falls, at least when I went in summer, is that the foliage is so tight that it's hard to get a good look at the entire falls, much less take a good picture of it. It's beautiful, for sure. You just have to digest it in pieces.

The hike is just a mile, round-trip, if you stay at the top of the falls. I explored a bit more down below the falls—that's why my hike registered at just under 1.4 miles.

*Just a few feet upstream of the falls, Lands Run is directed across the trail by culverts.*

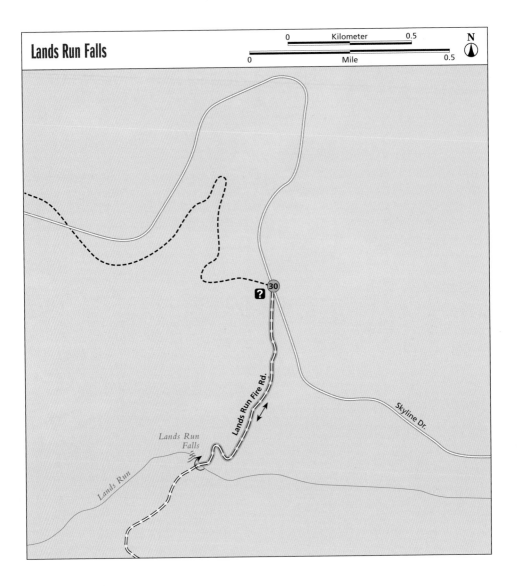

## Miles and Directions

**0.0**  Begin hiking south on the Lands Run Fire Road.

**0.5**  Arrive at the top of the falls (GPS: N38 49.696' / W78 11.347'), then retrace your steps to the trailhead.

**1.1**  Arrive back at the trailhead.

# 31 Overall Run Falls

The tallest waterfall in Shenandoah National Park—93 feet—waits for you at the end of this moderately strenuous hike. If you go in midsummer, there might not be much water in it, and you're actually hiking to an overlook across the Overall Run valley from the falls, but it's still worth the effort. After all, 93 feet is 93 feet.

**Height:** 93 feet
**Start:** The trailhead for the Traces Trail is at the north end of the amphitheater parking lot in the Mathews Arm Campground (right next to the campground check-in station).
**Distance:** 5.3 miles out and back
**Difficulty:** Moderate
**Canine compatibility:** Dogs must be on a 6-foot leash in Shenandoah National Park, but pets are not permitted on the Traces Trail.

**Trail surface:** Wide, mostly dirt path
**Hiking time:** 2-3 hours
**Blaze color:** Light blue
**County:** Warren
**Land status:** National Park
**Trail contact:** Shenandoah National Park: (540) 999-3500; nps.gov/shen. 3655 Highway 211 East, Luray 22835
**Maps:** *DeLorme, Virginia Atlas and Gazetteer:* page 74, B2

**Finding the trailhead:** To reach the trailhead in the Mathews Arm Campground, turn onto the access road between mileposts 22 and 23 on Skyline Drive. Park in the amphitheater parking lot. The trailhead for the Traces Trail is at the north end of the lot. **GPS:** N38 45.591' / W78 17.829'

## The Hike

This hike—the shortest way to Overall Run Falls—starts from the Mathews Arm Campground, which is open from May through October. To reach the falls the rest of the year, park at the lot just south of the Hogback Overlook between mileposts 21 and 22 on Skyline Drive. At the lower end of that lot, you'll find a trailhead for the Appalachian Trail. Go 0.4 mile on the AT, until you reach the Tuscarora Trail. Turn right onto that. It will eventually turn into the Tuscarora–Overall Run Trail, which will take you to the falls.

My hike started on the Traces Trail, which runs around the giant (217 camping spaces) Mathews Arm Campground. You won't be on that long, however. Once you reach the Tuscarora–Overall Run, you'll be on your way to the park's highest cataract. The going is relatively moderate by Shenandoah standards—not extremely steep or rocky until the last 0.2 mile.

This area of the park has a high concentration of black bears, so be on the lookout and don't be afraid: They won't bother you as long as you keep your distance and don't bother them.

You won't be alongside Overall Run for most of this hike. In fact, you may start wondering where the heck a waterfall could be because for a long time you don't hear

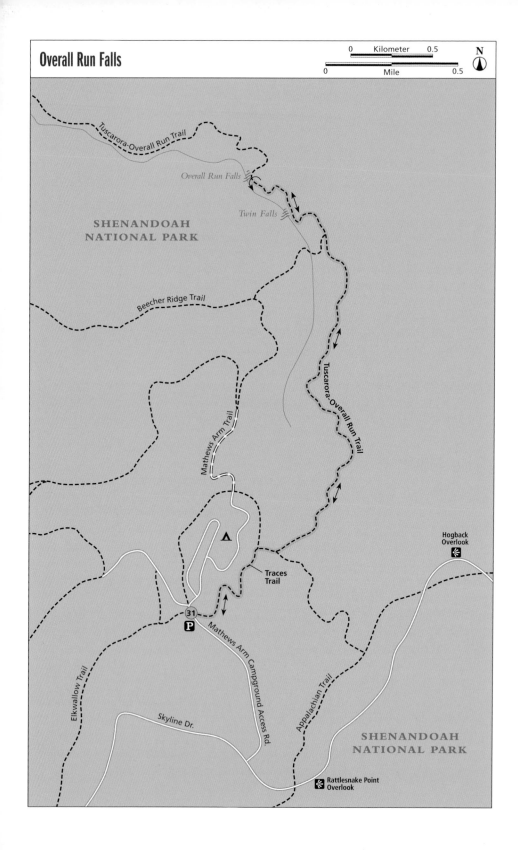

*In the heat of mid-summer, Overall Run Falls may not have much water in it.*

or see anything. But eventually Overall Run appears on your left, and at mile 2.2 you pass Twin Falls, where the creek splits around a big boulder and plunges about 25 feet. It's worth stopping here if you have the time to enjoy this shaded, woodland falls.

The big one—in fact, some people call it "Big Falls" instead of Overall Run Falls—is just 0.2 mile farther down the trail. If you go in the middle of July, like I did, you might be disappointed by how little water is pouring out of the falls. But the overlook has the added bonus of offering beautiful views of Massanutten Mountain and the Alleghenies in the distance. So there's really no bad time to make this hike.

## Miles and Directions

**0.0**  Begin hiking on the light-blue-blazed Traces Trail.

**0.5**  At a trail junction go right, staying on the Traces Trail for another 0.1 mile to another junction, where you'll find the Tuscarora-Overall Run Trail. Go left onto the Tuscarora-Overall Run Trail.

**2.0**  Mathews Arm Trail comes in from the left. Stay on Tuscarora-Overall Run Trail.

**2.2**  Pass Twin Falls, a small cascade of about 25 feet.

**2.6**  Arrive at Overall Run Falls (GPS: N38 46.986' / W78 17.626'), then retrace your steps to the trailhead.

**5.3**  Arrive back at the trailhead.

# 32 Hazel Falls

What's better than a waterfall hike? A waterfall-and-cave hike. Hazel Falls pours over and around a neat cave that's quite wide and deep. There are a couple of tempting swimming holes here as well. Hazel Falls may not be as well known as some other Shenandoah hikes, but it's one of my favorites.

**Height:** 25 feet
**Start:** The Hazel Mountain Trailhead is at the south end of the small parking area.
**Distance:** 5.1 miles out and back
**Difficulty:** Moderate/strenuous
**Canine compatibility:** Dogs must be on a 6-foot leash in Shenandoah National Park.
**Trail surface:** Mostly dirt and rock singletrack. Steep stone stair-steps at the end.

**Hiking time:** 2-3 hours
**Blaze color:** Yellow
**County:** Rappahannock
**Land status:** National Park
**Trail contact:** Shenandoah National Park: (540) 999-3500; nps.gov/shen. 3655 Highway 211 East, Luray 22835
**Maps:** *DeLorme Virginia Atlas and Gazetteer:* page 74, C2

**Finding the trailhead:** The Meadow Spring parking area is located on the east side of Skyline Drive between mileposts 33 and 34. **GPS:** N38 38.295' / W78 18.828'

## The Hike

When I arrived at the parking area to begin this hike, I looked at the hikers in the car next to me. Both were on smartphones, and I could see those familiar colors of radar maps with rain in the area. I guess I had been in space on my jaunt along Skyline Drive because I had no idea it was supposed to rain.

I heard the first clap of thunder as I set off down the Hazel Mountain Trail. I had rushed to get my gear together and get hiking, but now, with 5.1 miles ahead of me, I knew there'd be no outrunning the storm.

At the 0.4-mile mark, where the Buck Ridge Trail comes in, I reached for my water bottle—it was a muggy, warm day—but it wasn't there. *Oh, boy,* I thought. *This is not good. No water and I still have 4.5 miles of hiking to go. Not good at all.*

Then the rain came and saved me. It started pouring shortly thereafter and never let up. I caught the deluge in my hat and drank from that. It was a little salty at first from my sweat, but that was a small price to pay to have my thirst slaked.

It rained hard the entire walk down to Hazel Falls. The lightning and thunder were right on top of me, but there was nothing I could do, nowhere to go. Call me crazy, but it was kind of exhilarating.

Maybe all this colored my impression of Hazel Falls and the hike—in a good way—but I think I would have enjoyed this hike just as much in the middle of winter. When you arrive at the base of the Cave and Falls Trail, there's a gorgeous swimming

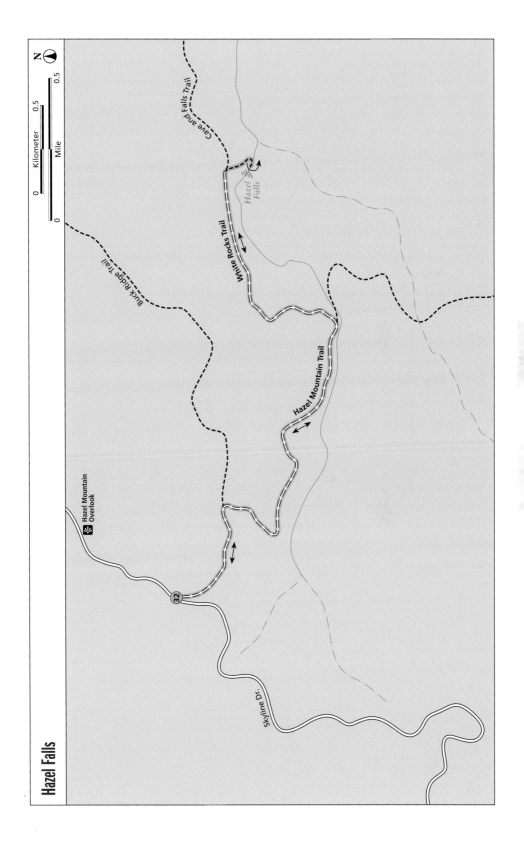

# Hazel Falls

Hazel Mountain Overlook

Hazel Mountain Trail

White Rocks Trail

Buck Ridge Trail

Cave and Falls Trail

Hazel Falls

Skyline Dr.

32

N

Kilometer
0          0.5

Mile
0          0.5

hole. Just upstream of that is Hazel Falls, sliding through a sluice beside a huge boulder. And under that boulder is the cave. If I weren't already soaked to the bone, this would have been a good place to wait out the storm.

Still, it was neat to turn on my phone's flashlight and check the place out. It's maybe 10 feet deep and 25 feet wide—good place to rest out of the sun on a hot day, eat lunch, and be tempted by the swimming hole in front of you.

The Hazel Falls hike has it all—a beautiful falls in a narrow valley and a cave alongside it, plus it's not too awfully strenuous. Put it on your list of Shenandoah National Park must-dos. Just check the radar before you go!

## Miles and Directions

**0.0**   Begin hiking on the Hazel Mountain Trail. (The concrete post at the trail calls it the Hazel Mountain "Road.")

**0.4**   The Buck Ridge Trail forks off to the left here. Stay on the Hazel Mountain Trail.

**1.6**   Go left onto the White Rocks Trail.

**2.4**   Turn right onto the Cave and Falls Trail.

**2.5**   Arrive at Hazel Falls (GPS: N38 38.080' / W78 17.181'), then retrace your steps to the trailhead.

**5.1**   Arrive back at the trailhead.

# SKYLAND

If you hike every Shenandoah National Park waterfall is this book, you'll drive all 105.6 miles of Skyline Drive. And over the course of that driving, the highest elevation you'll reach is 3,680 feet in the park's Central District (milepost 41.7). Here altitude meets history at the Skyland resort.

According to the National Park Service, "decades before Shenandoah National Park was established, vacationers traveled to Skyland Resort seeking respite from urbanized, mechanized city life. The resort was built in the late 1800s and grew in popularity among middle-class business people in nearby urban areas."

The dynamic George Freeman Pollock managed Skyland "with a showman's flair. His ever-present bugle awoke guests each morning, summoned them to meals and elaborate entertainments and announced the departure of the daily mail."

Skyland became part of the new Shenandoah National Park in 1937. And while many structures and spaces in the park were allowed to revert to a more natural state, much of Skyland was restored and maintained. Twelve historic structures remain, and today park visitors can eat at the Skyland restaurant and stay in one of 179 guest rooms, cabins, multiunit lodges, and modern suites.

Definitely put Skyland on your list of side trips while in the park, even if it's just to take in the view and grab a bite to eat.

# 33 Six Falls of Whiteoak Canyon

The Whiteoak Canyon hike is up there in Shenandoah National Park popularity with the Old Rag Mountain hike. It's not easy—that is for sure—but your effort is rewarded with not one but six distinct falls worthy of entry in this book, plus countless other smaller ones (complete with their own beautiful pools below them).

**Height:** (From top to bottom) no. 1: 86-foot cascade; no. 2: about 60 feet; no. 3: about 30 feet; no. 4: 40-foot slide; no. 5: 50 feet total in 2 sections; no. 6: 60 feet
**Start:** The trailhead is at the north end of the Whiteoak Canyon Parking Area.
**Distance:** 7.5 miles out and back
**Difficulty:** Strenuous
**Canine compatibility:** Dogs must be on a 6-foot leash in Shenandoah National Park.

**Trail surface:** Gravel at first, then rocky and steep
**Hiking time:** About 5 hours
**Blaze color:** Light blue
**County:** Madison
**Land status:** National Park
**Trail contact:** Shenandoah National Park: (540) 999-3500; nps.gov/shen. 3655 Highway 211 East, Luray, Virginia 22835
**Maps:** *DeLorme, Virginia Atlas and Gazetteer:* page 74, D2

**Finding the trailhead:** The Whiteoak Canyon Parking Area is on the east side of Skyline Drive between mileposts 42 and 43. **GPS:** N38 35.152' / W78 22.967'

*One of the toughest hikes in this book, Whiteoak Canyon rewards the intrepid waterfall hound with six beauties to take in. Here is the top falls.*

*The fourth falls in Whiteoak Canyon (starting from the top) offers an icy pool at the bottom for brave bathers.*

## The Hike

The Whiteoak Canyon falls hike may be exceedingly difficult in terms of cardiovascular effort, but it's pretty straightforward—at least until you get to the bottom.

You've got six falls on your docket, and they're all gorgeous in different ways. Whiteoak Canyon Trail starts off as a mostly smooth, hard-packed dirt surface. Around the 2-mile mark, you'll find falls number one, the tallest of the falls, and you'll also find that the trail steepens considerably. From here on out you'll be going down in a hurry, and if you're like me, you'll be thinking about coming back up this same steep trail.

*Falls number 5 requires some scrambling to get back up to from Falls number 6.*

Falls numbers two and three arrive quickly, then the next falls you'll see from the trail is falls number six. You will have passed falls number four and number five without realizing it. But that's OK because since you've had the legs under you to make it this far, you've probably got the strength left to scramble up to falls number five and then four.

To reach number five, look for the switchback in the trail just before the base of number six. From there you should see a trail, not an official one but one created by years of hikers doing what you're about to do. Take that trail and follow it upstream to the base of falls number five, a two-section cascade with an inviting swimming hole at the bottom. From the base of number five, rock-hop over Whiteoak Run (assuming

*Whiteoak Canyon's bottom falls is also its widest. There's plenty of room for swimming in the large hole here as well.*

the water isn't too high) and scramble steeply uphill on the left side of the falls to the base of number four.

Once you've taken in falls number four's 40 feet of steep-sliding watery beauty, you have two options: 1) You can retrace your steps, go back to the base of falls number six, and begin your ascent of Whiteoak Canyon, or 2) if you're like me, you won't want to waste the effort it took you to get to this point. Instead, you'll scramble uphill to the right of the falls until you find the trail. It's up to you, but know that if you choose the latter, you'll find the trail sooner rather than later.

Wherever you rejoin the trail, your work has only just begun. You've still got from 2.5 to 3 miles before you're back at the trailhead. Enjoy!

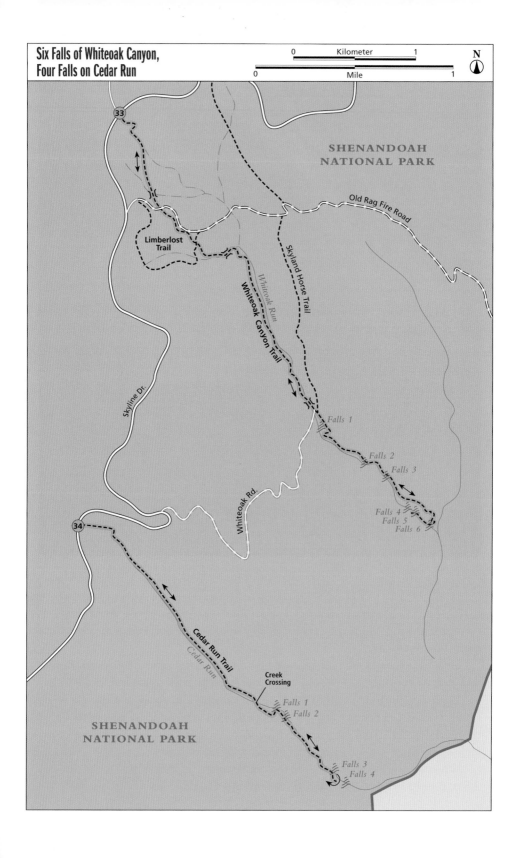

# Miles and Directions

**0.0** Whiteoak Canyon Trail begins at the trailhead at the north end of the parking lot.

**0.5** Arrive at the first bridge crossing over a creek. A few hundred feet later, cross Limberlost Trail. Then a few hundred feet after that, cross Old Rag Fire Road.

**0.8** Cross Limberlost Trail again.

**1.0** Cross Whiteoak Run for the first time on a bridge.

**1.9** Cross the creek on another bridge.

**2.0** Reach a trail junction with the Skyland Horse Trail. Just past the horse trail, the rocks with the best view of falls number one are off to the right (GPS: N38 33.800' / W78 21.797').

**2.4** Continue on the trail and arrive at falls number two (GPS: N38 33.636' / W78 21.542').

**2.6** Continue on the trail and arrive at an observation area above falls number three (GPS: N38 33.572' / W78 21.414').

**3.8** Continue on the trail and arrive at falls number six (GPS: N38 33.356' / W78 21.174').

**3.9** There's a switchback in the trail just before the base of falls number six. Above it you should see an unofficial path created from years of use. Follow it to the base of falls number five (GPS: N38 33.419' / W78 21.264').

**4.0** Cross the creek at the base of falls number five and scramble steeply uphill on the left side of the creek. You'll quickly find yourself at the base of falls number four (GPS: N38 33.413' / W78 21.285'). (**Options:** Either retrace your steps, going back down to falls number six and finding Whiteoak Canyon Trail, or cross the creek at the base of falls number four and scramble up the slope to the right of the falls and rejoin the trail somewhere along its length and hike uphill back to the trailhead.)

**7.5** Arrive back at the trailhead.

# 34 Four Falls on Cedar Run

It's a good thing Cedar Run cuts through such a gorgeous mountain valley with four beautiful waterfalls in it (and many more smaller cascades) because this is one tough hike. Bring your most rugged boots for this one.

**See map on page 108.**

**Height:** (From top to bottom) no. 1: 60 feet in series of slides; no. 2: 25-foot narrow chute; no. 3: 50 feet; no. 4: 35 feet through another chute

**Start:** The trailhead is on the east side of Skyline Drive at the north end of the gravel pull-off.

**Distance:** 4.5 miles out and back

**Difficulty:** Strenuous

**Canine compatibility:** Dogs must be on a 6-foot leash in Shenandoah National Park.

**Trail surface:** Very rocky almost the entire way

**Hiking time:** 3–4 hours

**Blaze color:** Light blue

**County:** Madison

**Land status:** National Park

**Trail contact:** Shenandoah National Park: (540) 999-3500; nps.gov/shen. 3655 Highway 211 East, Luray 22835

**Maps:** *DeLorme, Virginia Atlas and Gazetteer:* page 74, D2

**Finding the trailhead:** There are gravel pull-offs on either side of Skyline Drive at Hawksbill Gap between mileposts 45 and 46. Park on the east side, where the trailhead is. **GPS:** N38 33.362' / W78 23.195'

## The Hike

This hike has a lot in common with its neighbor, the six falls on Whiteoak Canyon. It's steep, it's relatively long (though not as long as Whiteoak), and it's almost arbitrary how many falls you decide there are in the canyon. I chose to pick four standouts. Let's just say, if you consider yourself a true waterfall hound, Cedar Run will not disappoint.

Here's another thing this hike has in common with Whiteoak: It's tough! In some ways, even though it's 3 miles shorter, it's even harder. That's because they both have about the same amount of elevation gain and loss—1,800 feet or so. Only Cedar makes you gain and lose that height in 4.5 miles. Whiteoak does so in over 7.5.

Cedar Run also makes you work harder for your footing. There's almost no simple, flat dirt or gravel tread. It's all a jumble of rocks.

Now that you're sufficiently impressed—or put off—you should know that to miss out on the waterfalls of Cedar Run is to miss one of the coolest places in the park. The canyon has an intimate feel. The canopy is relatively thick and the walls are close in.

There are innumerable pools for swimming and foot dipping, so no matter how hot you get, crystal-clear, icy-cold, mountain-stream relief is always just a few feet away.

I chose to count the series of cascades at the 1.5-mile mark as falls number one. Even though it leads directly to falls number two, it has a very different personality. At

*The first falls on Cedar Run is this dandy slide/swimming hole combo. Many hikers skip the remaining three falls because this one is so much fun.*

falls number one I watched kids ride the final flat granite slide into a pool on a hot summer day. Falls number two, by contrast, is a steep, narrow chute with a huge tree trunk stuck in the middle, and the pool below it was smaller and deeper. No sliding here, but it's striking in its own right.

Be careful at falls number three. You have to cross Cedar Run at the top of the falls and scamper down the granite face on the far side to reach the bottom. It's not terribly steep, but in high water this is not a place you want to slip and fall.

Falls number four has a similar character to number three, but here it's hard to reach the base because the near side, the bank right below you, is so steep. Both are far more easily enjoyed from the trail—unless, of course, you want to go swimming. Then you're on your own!

*Who knows how long this tree has sat lodged in Cedar Run Falls number 2?*

## Miles and Directions

**0.0** Begin at the trailhead for Cedar Run Trail at the north end of the gravel pull-off on the east side of Skyline Drive. Trees have light-blue blazes. Almost immediately you'll cross a horse trail. Stay straight on Cedar Run Trail.

**0.4** Cedar Run comes up alongside the trail for the first time.

**1.3** Cross the creek for the first time. There's a huge downed white oak across the stream on your left and a lovely small falls and pool on your right.

**1.5** Arrive at falls number one (GPS: N38 32.556' / W78 22.068'), a steep drop up top, then two long, flat cascades into popular swimming holes. Falls number two immediately follows the first (GPS: N38 32.548' / W78 22.043').

**1.9** Arrive at the top of falls number three (GPS: N38 32.277' / W78 21.757').

**2.2** Arrive at the top of falls number four (GPS: N38 32.235' / W78 21.694') and retrace your steps back to the trailhead.

**4.5** Arrive back at the trailhead.

# 35 Rose River Falls

The Rose River hike offers two falls, but they're so close together, one entry makes more sense. Reaching the lower drop requires a seriously dangerous scramble!

**Height:** Upper drop: 25 feet; lower drop: 40 feet
**Start:** You start at the north end of the overlook and then cross Skyline Drive to begin this hike on Rose River Fire Road.
**Distance:** 2.5 miles out and back
**Difficulty:** Moderate
**Canine compatibility:** Dogs must be on a 6-foot leash in Shenandoah National Park.
**Trail surface:** Rocky, narrow near falls

**Hiking time:** 1–2 hours
**Blaze color:** Yellow, then light blue
**County:** Madison
**Land status:** National Park
**Trail contact:** Shenandoah National Park: (540) 999-3500; nps.gov/shen. 3655 Highway 211 East, Luray 22835
**Maps:** *DeLorme, Virginia Atlas and Gazetteer:* page 74, D1

**Finding the trailhead:** Park at the Fishers Gap Overlook on the west side of Skyline Drive between mileposts 49 and 50. **GPS:** N38 32.046' / W78 25.324'

## The Hike

Rose River is more or less your standard Shenandoah woodland hike—rocky, not brutally steep, but not easy—until you reach the falls. I'll never cease to be amazed at how what seems like a little forest stream burbling over rocks can turn into a stunner of a waterfall.

This happens often with Virginia waterfalls, but it gets me every time.

Rose River is one of those. You're just hiking along, steadily downhill, enjoying the scenery, until you reach the precipice of the upper falls. As you take it in, realizing that the lower falls is crashing just downstream, all you can think is, "Wow! How did that small stream turn into those two gorgeous, powerful falls?"

The upper falls is smaller but also the better place for a picnic and to take pictures. Just to see the top of the lower falls, you've got to pick your way among some craggy rocks right next to a big drop-off. I scouted a possible scramble to the base of the lower falls, but with camera equipment on my back, I decided against it. Even if I had made it down, getting back up would have been tough. It's not necessary, though, to make it all the way to the bottom to enjoy this waterfall combo.

In addition to the falls themselves, there are rock cliffs across the river where water trickles from seeps and moss grows thick (at least in late winter). I imagine after a big rain, this would be a prime spot to sit and watch a torrent of water exit this tiny creek valley.

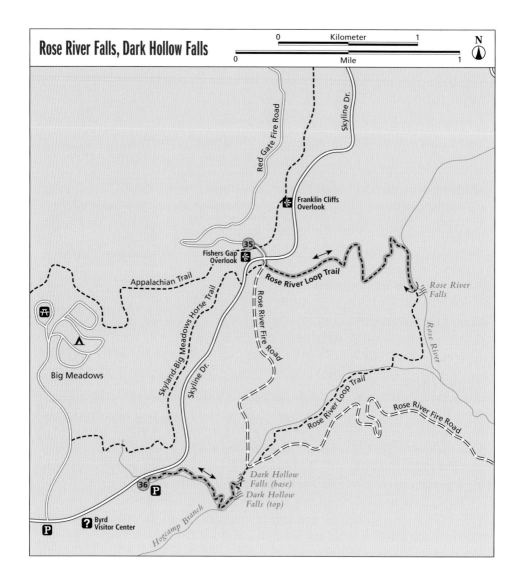

**Rose River Falls, Dark Hollow Falls**

## Miles and Directions

**0.0** From Fishers Gap Overlook, cross over Skyline Drive, briefly hike down the Rose River Fire Road, then make a left onto the Skyland/Big Meadows Horse Trail / Rose River Loop Trail.

**0.5** A horse trail goes off to the left. Stay on Rose River Loop Trail, which now has light-blue blazes.

**1.3** Arrive at the base of the upper falls/top of the lower falls (GPS: N38 31.889' / W78 24.513'), then retrace your steps to the trailhead.

**2.5** Arrive back at the trailhead.

# TROUT FISHING IN SHENANDOAH NATIONAL PARK

The eastern brook trout is the only trout species native to Virginia, and the headwater streams of Shenandoah National Park are a great place to seek out this gorgeous mountain dweller. President Herbert Hoover knew this. That's why he had his retreat, Rapidan Camp, built where the Mill and Laurel prongs come together to form the Rapidan River.

Hoover was a dedicated angler, and to this day the Rapidan is one of the best places to find brook trout in the park.

Shenandoah has over seventy fishable trout streams pouring off both sides of its crest. Some of those streams, like the Rose, are also great waters to ply for trout. One of my favorite things to do on my waterfall hikes is to bring along a fly rod and create a kind of three-for-one outdoor adventure: hiking, waterfall hounding, and fishing.

If you like to fly-fish but you've never been to Shenandoah National Park, a great way to get acquainted with the park's streams is to hire a guide. The park website (nps.gov/shen/planyourvisit/fishing.htm) has a list of permitted guides that you can find here.

Local fly-fishing expert Harry Murray says that early spring may be the best time to fish for brook trout in the park because of the high-quality early season insect hatches. Once water temperatures hold at highs of 40°F for a few days in a row, brook trout will start feeding on hatching mayflies.

"While large watersheds take some time to warm in the spring," Murray writes, at flyfisher man.com, "these small streams react quickly to a change to warmer weather. If the streams are high at low elevations, you can still find clear water and good fishing by parking on Skyline Drive and hiking down the trails to fish the upper sections of the streams. Or you can start at the lower park boundary and hike several miles upstream to get above the high water."

So, if it's your inclination, bring a fly rod with you on your next Shenandoah National Park waterfall hike and seek out the beautiful, elusive, native brook trout.

# 36 Dark Hollow Falls

The most popular waterfall hike in Shenandoah National Park isn't terribly long, but it is steep and can be a surprising lung buster.

**See map on page 114.**

**Height:** About 50 feet in multiple drops

**Start:** The trailhead is at the northwest end of the parking area, near the edge of Skyline Drive.

**Distance:** 1.5 miles out and back

**Difficulty:** Moderate

**Canine compatibility:** Dogs must be on a 6-foot leash in Shenandoah National Park.

**Trail surface:** Wide, hard-packed gravel

**Hiking time:** About 45 minutes

**Blaze color:** None

**County:** Madison

**Land status:** National Park

**Trail contact:** Shenandoah National Park: (540) 999-3500; nps.gov/shen. 3655 Highway 211 East, Luray 22835

**Maps:** *DeLorme, Virginia Atlas and Gazetteer:* page 74, D1

**Finding the trailhead:** The parking area is on the east side of Skyline Drive between mileposts 51 and 52 just north of Big Meadows. **GPS:** N38 31.182' / W78 25.852'

## The Hike

You'll almost never have this hike, or the falls, to yourself, but it's still worth putting on your Shenandoah National Park to-do list, especially if you're staying in the Big Meadows area. The trail starts at the north end of the large parking lot with a bridge over Hogcamp Branch. Follow it downhill on the wide hard-packed dirt and gravel path.

Hogcamp Branch isn't more than a rivulet in many places, but it eventually builds enough that just before the half-mile mark, you'll find a series of slides dropping into a nice little swimming hole/pool. If the hike were longer or the footing more treacherous, I'd give this a "moderate/strenuous" rating, because there's plenty of elevation change. My GPS registered 500 feet of drop from the trailhead to the base of the falls. And, of course, what goes down must hike back up.

When you reach the falls, you'll find a lovely series of cascades crashing onto and over granite outcroppings. It's the kind of falls that invites you to go exploring among those drops and boulders. Considering the crowds you're likely to find, you may even see people doing that. *A word of advice:* Be very careful. There's plenty of danger at Dark Hollow, even if the fifty people around you don't seem to notice it.

*No matter when you go, you won't have Dark Hollow Falls to yourself, but it's worth the trip anyway.*

## Miles and Directions

**0.0**  Start at the north end of the parking lot and cross Hogcamp Branch. The trail stays alongside the creek for the entire hike.

**0.5**  A series of slides ends in a nice, deep pool.

**0.6**  Reach the top of the falls. Continue down steeply to the bottom of the falls.

**0.7**  Reach the bottom of the falls (GPS: N38 31.152' / W78 25.397'), then retrace your steps to the trailhead.

**1.5**  Arrive back at the trailhead.

# 37 Lewis Falls

This is one of the most popular—and highest—falls in Shenandoah National Park due to its proximity to the Big Meadows Lodge area and its amphitheater shape.

**Height:** 80 feet
**Start:** The trailhead is in the lot on the west side of Skyline Drive at milepost 51.4 and is well marked.
**Distance:** 1.8 miles out and back
**Difficulty:** Moderate/strenuous
**Canine compatibility:** Dogs must be on a 6-foot leash.
**Trail surface:** Service road is hard-packed gravel; singletrack is rocky and rooty

**Hiking time:** About 1 hour
**Blaze color:** Light blue
**County:** Page
**Land status:** National Park
**Trail contact:** Shenandoah National Park: (540) 999-3500; nps.gov/shen. 3655 Highway 211 East, Luray 22835
**Maps:** DeLorme, Virginia Atlas and Gazetteer: page 74, D1

**Finding the trailhead:** Park in the lot on the west side of Skyline Drive at milepost 51.4 just before or just after Tanners Ridge Overlook, depending on which direction you're coming from. **GPS:** N38 31.024' / W78 26.519'

## The Hike

Shenandoah National Park specializes in hikes and falls like this one—steep, relatively short woodland hikes with multiple creek crossings that end at what I call "amphitheater falls," where the forest opens up at the top of the falls, the water drops off a lip, and you're wowed by a view of the valley below in addition to the view of the falls.

The hike to Lewis Falls (sometimes called Lewis Spring Falls) starts at a small lot along Skyline Drive. I thought about giving it a more difficult rating, but it's short enough that "moderate/strenuous" is probably correct, even though it's steep in places. Start on the gravel road at the lot's north end and head downhill. A third of a mile in, you'll pass Lewis Spring, then an old pump house (with a cool wooden door), then you'll see the junction with the Lewis Falls Trail. The trail crosses Hawksbill Creek a couple of times and makes a few switchbacks. At 0.8 mile stay left to reach the overlook.

You can't see the whole falls from the stone overlook, but you can see most of it. A bushwhack to the bottom to see the whole thing is not recommended in this steep creek valley. This overlook is a great place to relax, have a bite to eat, and take in the dual-viewing options of this hike.

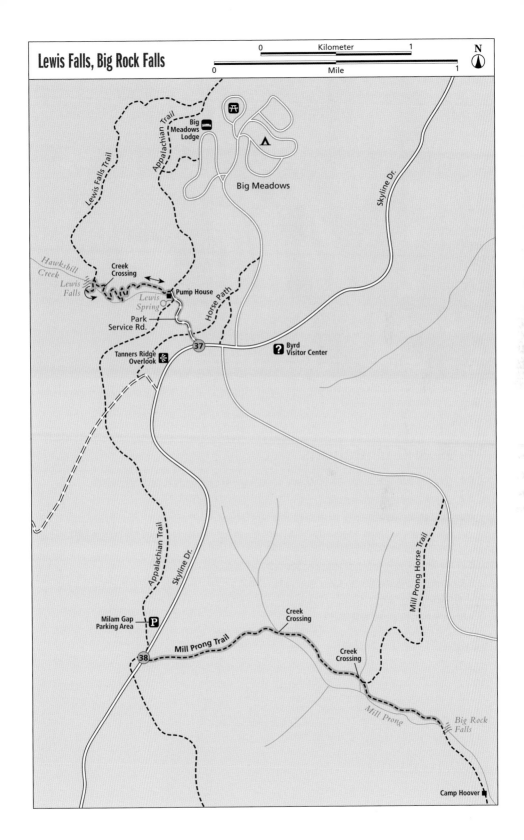

# Lewis Falls, Big Rock Falls

0 Kilometer 1

0 Mile 1

N

**Big Meadows Lodge**

*Hawksbill Creek*

Lewis Falls Trail

Appalachian Trail

Big Meadows

Skyline Dr.

Creek Crossing

*Lewis Falls*

Pump House

*Lewis Spring*

Horse Path

Park Service Rd.

37

Byrd Visitor Center

Tanners Ridge Overlook

Appalachian Trail

Skyline Dr.

Mill Prong Horse Trail

Milam Gap Parking Area

P

Creek Crossing

38

Mill Prong Trail

Creek Crossing

*Mill Prong*

*Big Rock Falls*

Camp Hoover

*The hike to Lewis Falls is short but steep and, because of its central location in Shenandoah National Park, usually crowded.*

## Miles and Directions

**0.0** At the north side of the gravel lot, you'll find a gravel service road leading downhill.

**0.2** Cross the Appalachian Trail.

**0.3** Still on the service road, you'll see Lewis Spring on your left and then, immediately after, an old pump house on your right. Just past the pump house, you'll see the double light-blue blazes indicating a trail junction. Take the trail to the left.

**0.7** Arrive at Lewis Falls Trail junction. Stay left and cross the creek.

**0.9** Arrive at the overlook to Lewis Falls (GPS: N38 31.221' / W78 26.977'), then retrace your steps.

**1.8** Arrive back at the trailhead.

# WHERE DID ALL THE EASTERN HEMLOCKS GO?

Throughout Shenandoah National Park, but especially on the waterfall hikes in Whiteoak Canyon and along Cedar Run, you'll notice a huge number of standing dead evergreen trees. Those trees are most likely eastern hemlocks.

Once, along with American chestnuts, eastern hemlocks dominated cool, wet mountain forests in the Southeast. But then came the hemlock woolly adelgid, a tiny insect native to Japan and China that was introduced to the western United States in the 1920s. The insects kill eastern and Carolina hemlocks, which have no natural defense against the nonnative pest, by feeding on the sap at the base of hemlock needles. This disrupts nutrient supplies to the foliage and causes the needles to change from deep green to a grayish green and then fall off. Without needles, the tree starves to death, usually within three to five years of the initial attack.

According to the US Fish and Wildlife Service:

> The hemlock wooly adelgid was first detected in the eastern U.S. in Richmond in the 1950s, where it began to spread rapidly, west into the Blue Ridge . . . Hemlock woolly adelgid currently infests about one-half of the area where hemlocks grow in the eastern U.S. Eighty percent of the hemlocks in Virginia's Shenandoah National Park are now dead. With them goes habitat for birds—many of them neotropical migrants that only nest in hemlock branches. Other forest birds will also be affected: in one study, 96 percent of all wood thrush nests found by surveyors were in hemlocks. Hemlocks help cool the mountain streams that are home to trout and other native fish, as well as crawfish, salamanders, and numerous aquatic insects. Foresters warn of a potential disaster comparable to the chestnut blight, which eliminated chestnut trees from the Southern Appalachian landscape and radically changed the composition of the forests of the Southeast.

There are ways to treat the infestation in affected trees but they're cost-prohibitive on a large scale. So, as you hike, enjoy the towering hemlocks you see offering shade and homes for wildlife, as they might not be there forever.

# 38 Big Rock Falls (SNP)

One of two "Big Rock Falls" entries in this book, this one is a modest slide but a worthy hike in Shenandoah National Park.

**See map on page 119.**
**Height:** 12-foot slide
**Start:** The trailhead, where you pick up the Appalachian Trail ever so briefly, is at the south end of the Milam Gap parking area.
**Distance:** 3.1 miles out and back
**Difficulty:** Easy/moderate
**Canine compatibility:** Dogs must be on a 6-foot leash in Shenandoah National Park.
**Trail surface:** Rocky, rooty, but not steep

**Hiking time:** 1–2 hours
**Blaze color:** Light blue, then yellow
**County:** Madison
**Land status:** National Park
**Trail contact:** Shenandoah National Park: (540) 999-3500; nps.gov/shen; 3655 Highway 211 East, Luray 22835
**Maps:** DeLorme, Virginia Atlas and Gazetteer: page 68, A1

**Finding the trailhead:** The trail starts at the Milam Gap Parking Area on the west side of Skyline Drive, between mileposts 52 and 53. **GPS:** N38 30.011' / W78 26.754'

## The Hike

Big Rock won't be the most impressive falls you see in Shenandoah National Park, so it's kind of nice that this isn't the hardest hike either. Maybe you're just not quite feeling up to one of the longer, steeper waterfall hikes the park is known for. With Big Rock, you won't get the payoff of a Whiteoak Canyon or South River—not even close—but you will get a more moderate grade for a hike through a beautiful woodland setting, next to a creek strewn with mossy boulders.

You park at Milam Gap, but then immediately cross back over Skyline Drive on the Appalachian Trail to get to Mill Prong Trail. You won't hear or see Mill Prong (the creek, not the trail) until about 0.6 mile into the hike, then you'll soon have to rock-hop across it, which should be no problem unless it's just rained. You'll have one more creek crossing, this time of a side creek, before a trail junction greets you. Here the Mill Prong Horse Trail comes in. You want to stay on it downhill following the water.

At 1.5 miles into your hike, you'll see a series of small drops before you reach Big Rock Falls. There's nothing really "big" about it, unless you count the large amount of serenity to be gained from sitting on one of the mossy rocks nearby taking in the beauty of the place. And if you're feeling adventurous, keep hiking another 0.4 mile to Camp Hoover, aka Rapidan Camp, the historic former retreat of President Herbert Hoover.

# Miles and Directions

**0.0** Cross Skyline Drive on the Appalachian Trail, then make an immediate left (following signs) onto light-blue-blazed Mill Prong Trail.

**0.7** Cross Mill Prong for the first time (easy rock-hop).

**1.0** Cross a different creek this time as it comes close to joining Mill Prong.

**1.1** Shortly after the creek crossing, Mill Prong Horse Trail comes in. Stay on that as blazes change from light blue to yellow. Go downhill, following the sound of the creek.

**1.6** Arrive at the base of the falls (GPS: N38 29.725' / W78 25.432'), then retrace your steps to the trailhead. (*Option:* To get to Camp Hoover [aka Rapidan Camp], the historic former retreat of President Herbert Hoover, keep hiking another 0.4 mile.)

**3.1** Arrive back at the trailhead.

# CAMP HOOVER

If you plan on hiking to Big Rock Falls, it's less than half a mile farther down Mill Prong Trail to one of Shenandoah National Park's most famous historical remnants. And considering Big Rock Falls is lovely but not the most impressive waterfall in the park, it's worth it to keep hiking to Camp Hoover, aka Rapidan Camp.

The official name of the site, Rapidan Camp, is explained by the two streams—Mill Prong and Laurel Prong—that come together to form the Rapidan River on the property.

The second name comes from Herbert Hoover, thirty-first president of the United States, who used it as a summer weekend retreat in 1929, during the early days of his administration.

According to the National Park Service, which maintains the rustic cabins on the site, the camp provided Hoover and his wife, Lou Henry, rest and recreation during the later difficult years of his presidency, after the stock market crash in October 1929.

The 164-acre property was secluded among the hemlocks on the eastern slope of the Blue Ridge Mountains, and included thirteen cabins. The natural setting was enhanced by rock gardens, waterfalls, and other stone structures. Here, the NPS reports, "the Hoovers entertained family members, friends, Cabinet officers, and politicians for relaxing weekends of hiking, horseback riding, and fishing. Hoover also used the camp as an informal setting for planning sessions with his cabinet and for private meetings with representatives of foreign governments."

The Hoovers donated Rapidan Camp to the Commonwealth of Virginia in 1932 for use as a summer retreat for subsequent presidents. It officially became part of Shenandoah National Park in 1935. Jimmy Carter was the last president to use the camp, in the late 1970s.

# 39 South River Falls

South River Falls is one of my absolute favorites in this book, as much for the hike as the falls. Both are spectacular. Put it on your list of Shenandoah National Park must-dos.

**Height:** 83 feet
**Start:** The trailhead is located at the east end of the South River Picnic Area.
**Distance:** 2.8 miles out and back
**Difficulty:** Moderate/strenuous
**Canine compatibility:** Dogs must be on a 6-foot leash in Shenandoah National Park.
**Trail surface:** Wide, rocky trail
**Hiking time:** 1–2 hours

**Blaze color:** Light blue
**County:** Greene
**Land status:** National Park
**Trail contact:** Shenandoah National Park: (540) 999-3500; nps.gov/shen. 3655 Highway 211 East, Luray 22835
**Maps:** *DeLorme, Virginia Atlas and Gazetteer:* page 67, A7

**Finding the trailhead:** The trailhead is located at the east end of the South River Picnic Area, between mileposts 62 and 63 on Skyline Drive. **GPS:** N38 22.866' / W78 31.011'

*Between the drama of this waterfall and the enchanting hike to it, the South River Falls experience is one of the best in Virginia.*

# The Hike

South River Falls, at 83 feet, is the third-tallest waterfall in Shenandoah National Park. It's impressive, and the views of the falls and the valley below are gorgeous, but what truly sets this falls apart is the hike to get there.

What starts as your standard forest hike changes about 0.6 mile in. Here you pick up the South River and the trail follows it to the falls. But the South River cuts a wider path through this mountain valley than most streams up on the Blue Ridge Mountains. The result is the feeling of walking along a dozen creeks taking different paths to the head of the falls. The South's many arms burble past mossy boulders and countless downed trees, all slick and covered with lichens and ferns. If you have the time, stop and explore before or after you reach the falls.

Once you reach the overlook, you'll realize you can see most but not all of South River Falls. To get to the bottom, follow the trail a few hundred yards past the overlook, turn right onto a forest road, and hike down half a mile to the river. You'll then have to hike upstream along a tiny trail to the base of the falls. If you enjoy a good strenuous hike, this is a nice little addition. If not, stay at the overlook and take in the sweeping views and amphitheater effect that South River Falls offers.

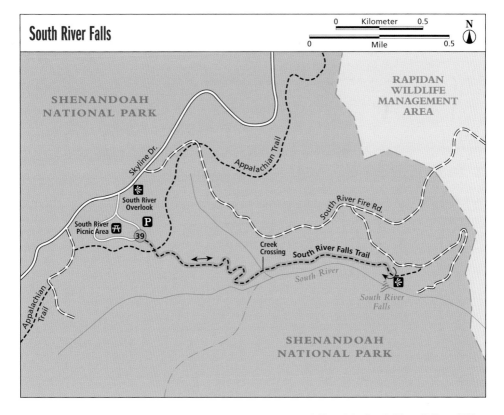

# Miles and Directions

**0.0** Follow light-blue blazes at the trailhead at South River Picnic Area.

**0.1** Cross the Appalachian Trail.

**0.6** The trail begins to parallel South River.

**1.2** Cross a creek that joins from the left.

**1.4** Arrive at the falls overlook (GPS: N38 22.773' / W78 29.988'), then retrace your steps to the trailhead. (**Option:** To see all of the South River falls, follow the trail a few hundred yards past the overlook, turn right onto a forest road, and hike down half a mile to the river. From here, hike upstream along a tiny trail to the base of the falls.)

**2.8** Arrive back at the trailhead.

# 40 Two Waterfalls on Doyles River

A popular hike that passes two sets of intimate woodland cascades, each with a personality of its own. This one is often paired with Jones Run Falls for a longer loop hike.

**Height:** Upper Falls: 3 cascades, 30 feet total; Lower Falls: 60 feet of steep cascades
**Start:** The trailhead is obvious at the small Doyles River Parking Area on Skyline Drive.
**Distance:** 3.1 miles to the lower falls and back
**Difficulty:** Moderate
**Canine compatibility:** Dogs must be on a 6-foot leash in Shenandoah National Park
**Trail surface:** Wide, rocky trail; narrow, steep, and rocky between the 2 falls

**Hiking time:** 1–2 hours
**Blaze color:** Light blue
**County:** Albemarle
**Land status:** National Park
**Trail contact:** Shenandoah National Park: (540) 999-3500; nps.gov/shen; 3655 Highway 211 East, Luray 22835
**Maps:** *DeLorme, Virginia Atlas and Gazetteer:* page 67, C6

**Finding the trailhead:** The trailhead is located at the Doyles River Parking Area on the east side of Skyline Drive between mileposts 81 and 82. **GPS:** N38 15.251' / W78 40.974'

## The Hike

One of the most popular circuit hikes in Shenandoah National Park combines the Jones Run Trail, Doyles River Trail, and the Appalachian Trail in a big loop of almost 7 miles. If you're up for a longer day, that hike will allow you to bag three waterfalls for the price of one. If you don't have as much time (or energy), both Jones Run Falls and the two falls on Doyles River are worth the expenditure.

This hike is not unlike the Jones Run Falls hike: Start at the parking area on Skyline Drive; hike steeply downhill through forest; level out a bit and begin following the stream; arrive at the falls. There are differences, though. The early steep section is steeper on Doyles River Trail, and the flatter section paralleling the river is wider and more open. Both offer that sense of anticipation you get on a waterfall hike when you can just feel—and then barely hear—the falls in the distance.

Another thing that separates Doyles River is the amount of downed eastern hemlocks choking the stream. There are times when you'll be walking right next to the creek and barely be able to see it because of all the dead trees. The dreaded and invasive hemlock woolly adelgid has decimated eastern hemlock populations throughout Shenandoah NP.

Even though it requires a steep and slightly treacherous final 0.1 mile of scrambling to reach, make sure to take in the lower Doyles River Falls. It's the higher and more impressive of the two.

# Two Waterfalls on Doyles River, Jones Run Falls

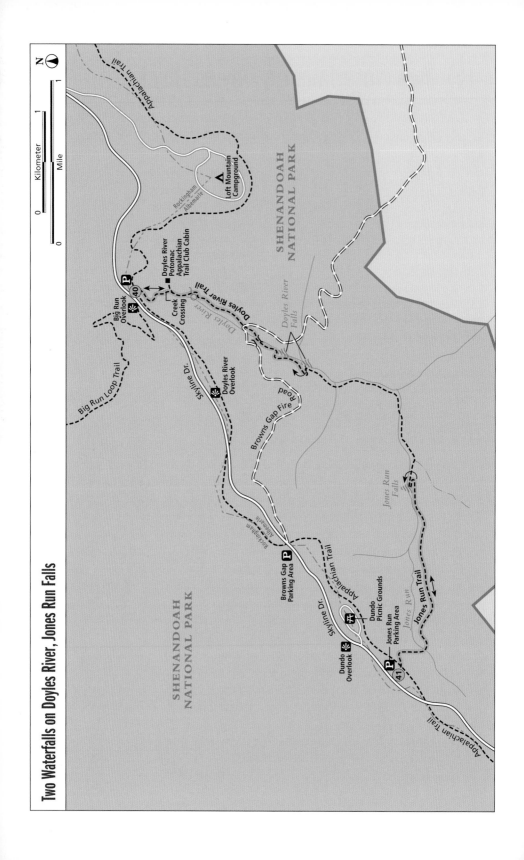

*Make a challenging, and rewarding, circuit hike out of Jones Run and Doyles River Falls. Pictured here is the upper falls on Doyles River.*

## Miles and Directions

**0.0** Start at the south end of the Doyles River Parking Area and soon pass the Appalachian Trail.

**0.3** Cross Doyles Spring and the side trail to access the Potomac Appalachian Trail Club's Doyles River Cabin.

**0.7** The trail begins to parallel the river.

**0.9** Cross Browns Gap Fire Road.

**1.0** Cross Doyles River on a wooden bridge.

**1.2** Arrive at the upper falls (GPS: N38 14.428' / W78 41.408').

**1.5** Arrive at the top of the lower falls.

**1.6** Arrive at the base of the lower falls (GPS: N38 14.328' / W78 41.471'), then retrace your steps to the trailhead.

**3.1** Arrive back at the trailhead.

# 41 Jones Run Falls

This is one of the Shenandoah National Park classics because of its relative ease in reaching and the lush rock wall covered in ferns over which it pours. In winter that rock wall is often completely covered in ice.

**See map on page 128.**
**Height:** Nearly sheer drop of about 40 feet
**Start:** The Jones Run Parking Area is small, and the trailhead will be obvious at the south end.
**Distance:** 3.7 miles to the lower falls and back
**Difficulty:** Moderate/strenuous
**Canine compatibility:** Dogs must be on a 6-foot leash.
**Trail surface:** Wide, rocky trail

**Hiking time:** 1–2 hours
**Blaze color:** Light blue
**County:** Albemarle
**Land status:** National Park
**Trail contact:** Shenandoah National Park: (540) 999-3500; nps.gov/shen. 3655 Highway 211 East, Luray 22835
**Maps:** *DeLorme, Virginia Atlas and Gazetteer:* page 67, C6

**Finding the trailhead:** The trailhead is located at the Jones Run Parking Area on the east side of Skyline Drive between mileposts 84 and 85. **GPS:** N38 13.797' / W78 43.565'

*Jones Run Falls is breathtaking in any season.*

# The Hike

One of the most popular circuit hikes in Shenandoah National Park combines the Jones Run Trail, Doyles River Trail, and the Appalachian Trail in a big loop of almost 7 miles. If you're up for a longer day, that hike will allow you to bag three waterfalls for the price of one. If you don't have as much time (or energy), both Jones Run Falls and the two falls on Doyles River are worth the expenditure.

You'll appreciate the combination of power and intimacy at Jones Run Falls. There are a couple of good-size drops to enjoy before you reach the main one, but when you do you'll want to stay there a while, feeling the mist on your skin as the water thunders over a nearly vertical 40-foot rock wall. Not many falls in Shenandoah National Park are big and powerful and allow you to easily reach the base. Take advantage of this one.

## Miles and Directions

**0.0**   Start hiking downhill on light-blue-blazed Jones Run Trail.

**0.1**   Cross the Appalachian Trail.

**0.6**   Cross Jones Run. The trail begins to flatten out some here.

**1.7**   Arrive at the top of the falls.

**1.8**   Arrive at the base of the falls (GPS: N38 13.773' / W78 42.283'), then retrace your steps to the trailhead.

**3.7**   Arrive back at the trailhead.

# 42 Waterfall on Big Branch

The locally renowned "Blue Hole" is nearby on the South Fork Moormans River, but a hike up the North Fork Moormans—and then at the end along tiny Big Branch—rewards hardy waterfall seekers with creek crossings, swimming holes, and a few smaller drops before reaching the impressive upper falls.

**Height:** 45 feet
**Start:** The first of 2 gravel parking lots at the end of Sugar Hollow Road. Reaching the second one requires a car with good clearance.
**Distance:** 4.2 miles out and back
**Difficulty:** Moderate/strenuous
**Canine compatibility:** Dogs must be on a 6-foot leash in Shenandoah National Park.
**Trail surface:** Hard-packed dirt, sometimes rocky

**Hiking time:** 1–2 hours
**Blaze color:** Yellow
**County:** Albemarle
**Land status:** National Park
**Trail contact:** Shenandoah National Park: (540) 999-3500; nps.gov/shen; 3655 Highway 211 East, Luray 22835
**Maps:** DeLorme, Virginia Atlas and Gazetteer: page 67, C6

**Finding the trailhead:** From I-64, about 15 miles west of Charlottesville, get off on exit 107 and turn right onto US 250 heading east. In the town of Brownsville, turn left and go north on SR 240 (Crozet Avenue). Take SR 240 through the town of Crozet and turn right on SR 810 (White Hall Road). At the town of White Hall, turn left onto SR 614 (Sugar Hollow Road) heading west. Follow Sugar Hollow Road up to and past the Charlottesville Reservoir (aka Sugar Hollow Reservoir) until you find the gravel parking lot. **GPS:** N38 08.641' / W78 44.911'

## The Hike

There are two parking lots available at the end of Sugar Hollow Road. This hike starts at the first one—about a half mile before the second—because my car couldn't handle the rutted road in between. If you have four-wheel drive, though, you should be fine.

If you start where I did, you'll have to hike that first half mile. But that's no big deal because the scenery here is beautiful. The North Fork Moormans is off to your left, and hemlock trees—those that haven't been infected by the hemlock wooly adelgid—tower above you. You're in the Shenandoah National Park backcountry. You'll quickly feel far from civilization.

Follow the yellow-blazed North Fork Moormans River Trail, which starts at the second lot. Soon you'll cross the river, which is really more of a creek. At the second creek crossing, you may be tempted to stop and swim in a beautiful, deep hole through which you can see clear to the bottom. If you're hiking on a weekend in the summer, you probably won't be alone at the swimming hole. It's a popular place.

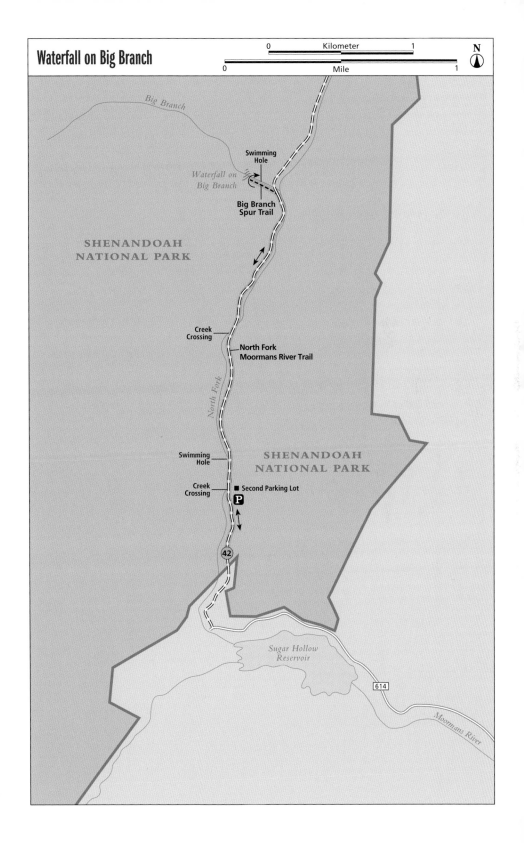

# Waterfall on Big Branch

Big Branch

Swimming Hole

*Waterfall on Big Branch*

Big Branch Spur Trail

SHENANDOAH NATIONAL PARK

Creek Crossing

North Fork Moormans River Trail

North Fork

Swimming Hole

SHENANDOAH NATIONAL PARK

Creek Crossing

■ Second Parking Lot

P

42

Sugar Hollow Reservoir

614

Moormans River

Keep going on the sometimes rooty, rocky trail. You'll pass many smaller falls, but you'll know you're nearing Big Branch and its waterfall when the trail steepens considerably. At this point, about 2 miles into your hike, the North Fork Moormans River Trail crosses Big Branch and goes off to the right. Don't take that. Instead, stay straight on the Big Branch Spur Trail. Stay on that for another 0.1 mile and you'll come to the base of the falls—a 45-foot waterslide that ends in a small pool.

*Note:* Be careful if you try to reach the top of the falls. It's very steep and moist up there, covered with lichens and moss. A fall up at the top would lead to serious injury.

## Miles and Directions

**0.0**   Start at the first of two possible trailheads. Depending on your vehicle and the recent weather, you might be able to drive on the rutted gravel road from the first parking area to a second one. I chose to stop at the first parking area and hike to the second.

**0.5**   The North Fork Moormans River Trail begins here at the second parking lot. Follow the yellow blazes. The trail parallels the creek upstream.

**0.8**   Cross the creek here for the first of a few times. The trail is always easy to find on the other side of the crossings. At the second creek crossing, a slightly more difficult one, there is also the first falls of the hike, a small slide that has a wonderful swimming hole at the base.

**1.6**   Cross the creek again.

**2.0**   The trail gets steeper here, and you know you're getting close. If you cross the creek here, you head off to the right on the North Fork Moormans River Trail. Stay straight and pay attention to the yellow blazes.

**2.1**   Arrive at the base of the falls (GPS: N38 09.968' / W78 44.784'). There are a few smaller cascades before you reach the upper falls. Return the way you came.

**3.7**   Pass the trailhead.

**4.2**   Arrive back at the parking lot.

# BLUE HOLE

The Waterfall on Big Branch isn't the only claim to fame for this area outside of Charlottesville. In fact, it's probably not the most famous claim. That honor goes to a place called Blue Hole, a swimming hole hugely popular with University of Virginia students and locals alike.

Whereas the hike to the Waterfall on Big Branch follows the North Fork Moormans River most of the way, the hike to Blue Hole, which starts at the same parking lot, follows the South Fork Moormans River. Both forks feed the Sugar Hollow Reservoir, which you passed on your way to the parking lot.

You're right at the edge of Shenandoah National Park here, but to reach Blue Hole, instead of following the road/trail you drove in on, follow the South Fork Moormans River Trail. There will be a cement post with a metal band pointing the way. You'll have to rock-hop across the river, and the trail continues on the other side. It's about a 1.5-mile hike to Blue Hole, which will be on your right.

If it's a hot summer day, you probably won't have the place to yourself, but Blue Hole is quite large and deep. There should be plenty of space. Whenever you go, be forewarned: This is Blue Ridge Mountain water you're talking about swimming in. It's cold no matter what time of year it is!

# 43 Riprap Run Falls

This is a sometimes overlooked gem due to its distance from Skyline Drive and the top of Shenandoah National Park. Riprap Run Falls offers the bonus of a gorgeous swimming hole.

---

**Height:** A series of falls, all about 5 feet high
**Start:** The trail and the Shenandoah National Park backcountry start on the other side of Meadow Run from where you parked.
**Distance:** 3.5 miles out and back
**Difficulty:** Easy/moderate
**Canine compatibility:** Dogs must be on a 6-foot leash in Shenandoah National Park.
**Trail surface:** Wide and rocky but hard-packed

**Hiking time:** 1–2 hours
**Blaze color:** Blue
**County:** Augusta
**Land status:** National Park
**Trail contact:** Shenandoah National Park: (540) 999-3500; nps.gov/shen; 3655 Highway 211 East, Luray 22835
**Maps:** *DeLorme, Virginia Atlas and Gazetteer:* page 67, C5

---

**Finding the trailhead:** From Skyline Drive at Rockfish Gap just east of Waynesboro, go west on US 250. Drive down the mountain 3.5 miles into the town of Waynesboro. Turn right on US 340. Stay on US 340 for 6.5 miles, then turn right on onto CR 612. Things get a little complicated back on these gravel county roads, so be patient. Go just over 1.5 miles on CR 612, then turn left onto Black Bear Lane. Almost immediately you'll come to a fork. Stay left onto Wild Turkey Lane and drive 1 mile to where it ends at a creek called Meadow Run. You'll see No Trespassing signs all over the place, but don't worry: You can park here. The trail starts just on the other side of Meadow Run, where the Shenandoah National Park backcountry begins. **GPS:** N38 09.476' / W78 48.710'

## The Hike

Up on Skyline Drive, at the Riprap Run Parking Area, you can set off on a 9.5-mile circuit hike that passes Riprap Run Falls. It's a beautiful day hike with great views in many different places, especially during the winter. But for the purposes of this book, I decided to focus on the fastest way to get to the falls.

This hike is a kind of mirror image to the one for the Waterfall at Big Branch. It's on the other side of the Blue Ridge, but they're both Shenandoah National Park backcountry hikes that start at the base of the mountains and go up. Most SNP hikes do the opposite. Neither hike is terribly steep, each closely parallels a stream, and both have awesome swimming holes available along the way.

Your hike starts with a stream crossing of Meadow Run, which in high water is not all that easy (unless you don't mind getting wet). Once across, follow the blue blazes on the Riprap Run Trail. Half a mile in you'll cross the eponymous stream (again, not easy in high water), and at the 1.1-mile mark the Wildcat Ridge Trail will come in on your right. Looking up at the ridge, you might be tempted to go that way—this is a gorgeous valley you'll hike through—but if you want to see the falls, keep going.

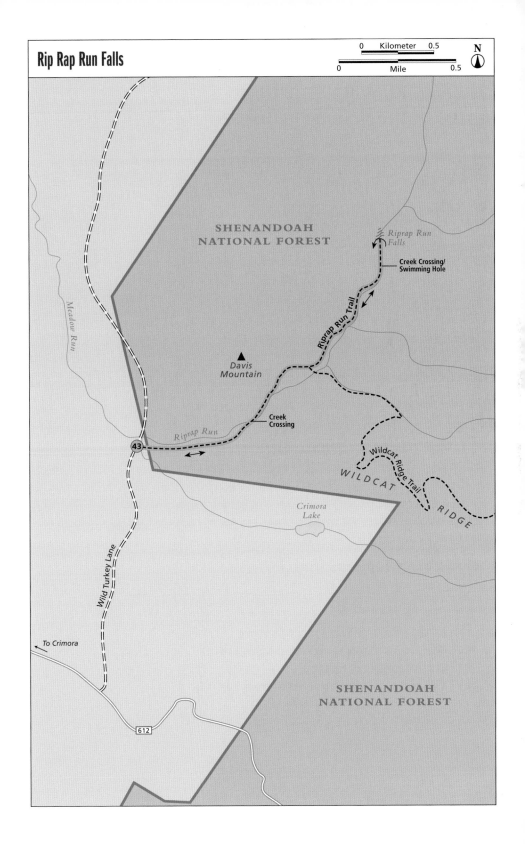

# Rip Rap Run Falls

0 Kilometer 0.5

0 Mile 0.5

N

SHENANDOAH
NATIONAL FOREST

Riprap Run
Falls

Creek Crossing/
Swimming Hole

*Meadow Run*

Riprap Run Trail

▲
*Davis
Mountain*

Creek
Crossing

43

*Riprap Run*

Wildcat Ridge Trail

WILDCAT

RIDGE

*Crimora
Lake*

Wild Turkey Lane

To Crimora

612

SHENANDOAH
NATIONAL FOREST

*Hike to Riprap Run Falls on a hot summer day and you won't be able to stay away from this deep pool just below the falls.*

Just over 1.5 miles in, you'll cross Riprap Run again and then you'll see the swimming hole. If it's hot out, you may have no choice but to swim here—it's that inviting. If it's cold, look down into the water and see if you can spy any native brook trout.

Above the swimming hole, you'll see a mounting number of smaller falls. The trail gets steeper here and you'll have one more creek crossing, then the trail arrives at the top of the falls.

## Miles and Directions

**0.0**  The trail begins on the other side of Meadow Run from where you parked.

**0.5**  Cross Riprap Run. The creek is now on your right.

**1.1**  Junction with Wildcat Ridge Trail, which comes in on the right.

**1.6**  Cross back over Riprap Run near the swimming hole.

**1.7**  Cross Riprap Run for a third time.

**1.8**  A short, steep section brings you up to the top of the falls (GPS: N38 10.202' / W78 47.589').

**3.5**  Arrive back at the parking area across Meadow Run.

# Piedmont

Geologically speaking, the Piedmont is the largest physiographic province in Virginia. It rubs up against the base of the Blue Ridge Mountains to the west and meets the Coastal Plain at its eastern border along what is commonly called the "Fall Line." Cities like Richmond (and others) exist where they do because explorers sailing up tidal rivers like the James could go no farther when they reached the rocky Fall Line.

The Piedmont is characterized by gently rolling topography and deeply weathered bedrock. That's why there are so few waterfalls here—not enough steepness or large, exposed rock outcrops. Even at the Fall Line, there's only one true waterfall worthy of an entry in this book—Great Falls—and that's up in the northern Virginia section for geographical reasons rather than geological ones.

Of the three waterfalls I've included in the Piedmont, only one is natural. The two in Richmond are almost directly across the James River from each other. But even if they aren't "real," they are falling water, and if you've opened this book, chances are you understand the power of falling water.

The one natural waterfall—the Falls of the Nottoway—is in the middle of nowhere and is absolutely worth the drive. In fact, its remote location, so far from anywhere you might think could harbor a waterfall, is what makes the place so special. If I had a list of the most surprising falls, that one would be near the top.

There are other, smaller falls in the Piedmont. There's one on the Newfound River north of Richmond, east of Kings Dominion, just off CR 685. I couldn't find a name for it, but it's small and I didn't think it was worth a separate entry. In the winter you should be able to see it from the road. There may be others as well, but if so, they are likely small and/or on private property.

The Piedmont isn't waterfall nirvana, but if you live in central Virginia or are traveling through, these three falls should whet your appetite for what awaits in the mountains.

# 44 Forest Hill Park Dam

The falls over the dam at Richmond's Forest Hill Park Lake can vary from a trickle to a torrent, depending on recent rainfall. When it's the latter, the thundering water is audible throughout the 100-acre wooded park.

**Height:** 12 feet
**Start:** The hike begins in the Reedy Creek Parking Lot of the James River Park System.
**Distance:** 1.0-mile lollipop
**Difficulty:** Easy
**Canine compatibility:** Dogs must be leashed in all Richmond city parks.
**Trail surface:** Hard-packed dirt and asphalt
**Hiking time:** About 25 minutes

**Blaze color:** None
**County:** City of Richmond
**Land status:** Public park
**Trail contacts:** Richmond Department of Parks, Recreation and Community Facilities: www .richmondgov.com/parks/; (804) 646-5733; 1209 Admiral Street, Richmond 23220
**Maps:** DeLorme, Virginia Atlas and Gazetteer: page 58, D2

**Finding the trailhead:** From the junction of SR 76 / Powhite Parkway and Forest Hill Avenue, about 5 miles southwest of downtown Richmond, drive east on Forest Hill Avenue 1.5 miles to 42nd Street. Turn left on 42nd Street and travel 0.3 mile to Riverside Drive. Turn right on Riverside Drive and drive 0.2 mile. The entrance to Reedy Creek Parking Lot/James River Park System is on the left. **GPS:** N37 31.400' / W77 28.249'

## The Hike

In some ways this hike, though short, is as rewarding as the dam and waterfall you've come for. From where you parked, hike back up the parking lot entrance. Richmond's famous Buttermilk Trail—popular with hikers, bikers, dog walkers, and birders—crosses the pavement here. Go left on Buttermilk, east toward Reedy Creek.

In no time you'll come to the small but often powerful creek. Enter the tunnels below Riverside Drive and hike upstream into Forest Hill Park, 105 acres of urban green space in the heart of the city. Go left up the trail on the creek bank and continue hiking upstream toward the falls. If you arrive in the middle of summer, the falls could be a trickle. Just after a rainstorm, it could be a deluge.

Follow the trail (now asphalt) above the falls and stay to the left of Forest Hill Park Lake. The city recently dredged what was a wetland, returning it to its 1920s-era glory when it was a popular swimming destination. Cross Reedy Creek on a sturdy metal bridge and turn right on the other side. The trail will loop back to the top of the dam and offers some peaceful time next to the lake.

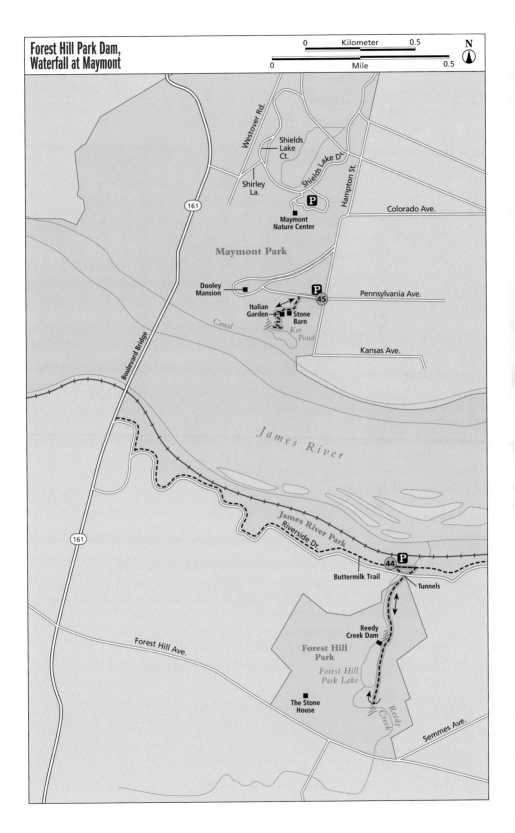

Kilometer

0                    0.5

Mile

0                    0.5

N

Westover Rd.

Shields
Lake
Ct.

Shields Lake Dr.

Shirley La.

Hampton St.

161

P

Colorado Ave.

Maymont
Nature Center

Maymont Park

Dooley
Mansion

P 45

Pennsylvania Ave.

Italian
Garden

Stone
Barn

Canal

Koi Pond

Kansas Ave.

Boulevard Bridge

James River

James River Park

Riverside Dr.

161

P 44

Buttermilk Trail

Tunnels

Reedy
Creek Dam

Forest Hill
Park

Forest Hill
Park Lake

Forest Hill Ave.

The Stone
House

Reedy Creek

Semmes Ave.

*The waterfall at the Forest Hill Park dam can be a trickle or a rushing torrent depending on recent rainfall.*

## Miles and Directions

**0.0** From the Reedy Creek Parking Lot and entrance to the James River Park System, hike back toward the parking lot's entrance. Follow signs east (left) onto Buttermilk Trail.

**0.1** Reedy Creek flows under Riverside Drive in two open tunnels to your right. Choose a tunnel and hike upstream (south) into Forest Hill Park. At the south end of the tunnels, get on the trail above you and continue hiking upstream.

**0.3** Arrive at base of Forest Hill Park Lake dam and falls (GPS: N37 31.212' / W77 28.284'). Here the trail becomes paved. Hike past the dam, staying on the left side of the lake.

**0.5** Cross Reedy Creek on a metal bridge. Follow the loop around the lake back to the dam and falls.

**1.0** Arrive back at the trailhead.

# "FALLS OF THE JAMES"

If you're familiar with the James River, you've probably heard people refer to the "Falls of the James." *Wait,* you might be wondering, *there's a waterfall on the James? Why isn't it in this book?*

Well, it's not a waterfall, per se. In the 7-mile stretch between Bosher's Dam at Richmond's western border to the Mayo Bridge downtown, the James drops 105 feet in elevation. This "Fall Line" is where the Piedmont to the west meets the Coastal Plain to the east. Above Richmond the James is shallow and rocky; below Virginia's capital it's deep and tidal.

So while there's no true waterfall in the Falls of the James, the elevation change does create the conditions for some of the nation's best urban whitewater paddling. Boaters regularly navigate Class IV whitewater at Hollywood and Pipeline rapids. No other urban area of its size can boast of better whitewater than Richmond.

If you'd like to see these dramatic stretches of turbulent water for yourself, you're in luck. You can sit on a rock at Belle Isle, a 90-acre island that's part of the James River Park System, and watch paddlers take on Hollywood. Or you can head downriver to Pipeline Park (also part of the JRPS) and do the same at Pipeline Rapid. These might not be waterfalls like you're used to seeing in the mountains, but they are a dramatic testament to the power of the James as it cuts through the Fall Line.

# 45 Waterfall at Maymont

Enjoy this short stroll through one of Richmond's most popular tourist destinations to the most improbable waterfall in this book.

**See map on page 141.**
**Height:** 45 feet
**Start:** This hike begins at the parking lot at Maymont's Hampton Street entrance.
**Distance:** 0.6 mile out and back
**Difficulty:** Easy
**Canine compatibility:** No dogs are allowed in Maymont Park.
**Trail surface:** Mostly paved; some hard-packed dirt

**Hiking time:** About 15 minutes
**Blaze color:** None
**County:** Richmond city
**Land status:** Public park operated by local nonprofit
**Trail contact:** Maymont; maymont.org; (804) 358-7166; 1700 Hampton Street, Richmond 23220
**Maps:** *DeLorme, Virginia Atlas and Gazetteer:* 58, D2

**Finding the trailhead:** From I-64/I-95, get off on exit 78, 3 miles from downtown Richmond, and drive south on Boulevard. Follow Boulevard through Byrd Park and past the Carillon, but before you reach the Boulevard Bridge, turn left onto Shirley Lane. Stay on Shirley briefly, then make a right onto Shields Lake Court overlooking Shields Lake. Follow Shields Lake Court around the lake. You'll see the entrance to Maymont Nature Center, but this isn't the entrance you're looking for. When this road reaches the end of Shields Lake, and before it begins to run alongside Swan Lake, bend right on Shields Lake Court, then make a quick right on Hampton Street. Follow Hampton 0.25 mile to Maymont's Hampton Street entrance. The parking lot is also the trailhead. **GPS:** N37 32.050' / W77 28.472'

## The Hike

Why is this the most improbable waterfall in the book? Because it's man-made. But man, is it impressive. Before Maymont was a public park, it was the private estate of Richmond's Dooley family. In 1912 they created a Japanese garden, of which this waterfall is the centerpiece. The water that powers the falls is pumped from the Kanawha Canal below Maymont and falls 45 feet or so before being pumped back up to its "source" at the Italian Garden.

A paved path from the parking lot heads west along a ridge at the top of the Maymont estate. When you see the three-story Stone Barn, make a left and follow the stone path downhill toward the Italian Garden.

The Maymont waterfall is shut off from about November to April, so the pipes that feed it don't crack from the cold. But in the summer you'll hear the rush of the falls when you reach the Italian Garden. Continue on the stone path next to the granite that the water tumbles over and head down to the Japanese Garden.

When the stone stairs deposit you at the Koi Pond, make a right and in just a few feet you'll be at the base of the falls. Take a moment to slow down and just watch the falls.

As Maymont's website says: "Descending into the Japanese Garden and entering through its distinct gates is like stepping onto a different continent. The space is cool, shaded and intimate. Sounds are muted and even children become more introspective and observant."

So true. Do yourself a favor and let the waterfall, the beating heart of Maymont's Japanese Garden, wash over you.

## Miles and Directions

**0.0** From the trailhead enter Maymont and follow the paved path. Buildings will be on your left and the grounds will drop off to your right.

**0.1** Just past the Stone Barn, take a left onto a stone path downhill toward the Italian Garden.

**0.2** At the Italian Garden you'll see where the "creek" that feeds Maymont's waterfall begins. Follow the stone stairs to the left of the rockslide that eventually becomes the waterfall down to the Koi Pond at bottom of the park.

**0.3** At the Koi Pond the path turns to hard-packed dirt and gravel. Make a right and the base of the waterfall is just a few feet away (GPS: N37 31.991' / W77 28.624'). Return the way you came.

**0.6** Arrive back at the trailhead.

## MAYMONT

One ancillary benefit of the hike to the Japanese Garden waterfall at Maymont is that you pass through much of the park getting there. Maymont is a true central Virginia gem. It would be worthy of a trip even if there weren't a cool man-made waterfall in the middle of it.

Maymont was once a private estate owned by James Henry and Sallie Dooley from 1893 to 1925. According to their wishes, the Gilded Age mansion and the 100 acres surrounding it were gifted to the people of Richmond upon their deaths. It's now city owned but operated by the nonprofit Maymont Foundation.

The waterfall is the centerpiece of the Japanese Garden area, but Maymont has much more to offer. There is an Italian Garden, an indoor petting zoo, outdoor animal exhibits, a nature center, and miles of trails. There are also over 200 species of trees and woody plants on the Maymont grounds.

For all those reasons, Maymont has become the largest visitor attraction in Richmond (outside of the vast James River Park System), drawing 537,137 visitors in 2013. So, if you go for the waterfall, make sure you stay for everything else Maymont has to offer.

# 46 Falls of the Nottoway

This falls would be worth the drive if it were in the mountains. In the middle of the Piedmont, not even on the Fall Line, it's a geological oddity begging to be explored, especially in the summer when the pools beneath each slide are most inviting.

**Height:** 35 feet in a series of slides
**Start:** On the right side—the downstream side—of the gravel lot, you'll see a gravel service road. The trail starts there.
**Distance:** 0.4 mile out and back
**Difficulty:** Easy
**Canine compatibility:** Leashed dogs allowed
**Trail surface:** Dirt singletrack
**Hiking time:** About 10 minutes

**Blaze color:** None
**County:** Lunenburg/Nottoway border
**Land status:** Public
**Trail contact:** Town of Victoria; info@victoriava .net; PO Box 1421, 1802 Main Street, Victoria 23974
**Maps:** *DeLorme, Virginia Atlas and Gazetteer:* page 46, D3

**Finding the trailhead:** From US 360 in Richmond drive south for about 54 miles (depending on where, exactly, you start in Richmond) to the intersection with SR 49. Get on SR 49 going south and drive 15.5 miles to where it crosses the Nottoway River. Look right, upstream, and you'll see a dam and the Nottoway Falls Reservoir. Look left, and you'll see the top of the falls.

Drive 0.1 mile past the bridge and turn right at a gravel road. You'll see signs for a public boat ramp. Drive a hundred yards or so and stay right at the fork in the gravel road.

Park in that big, open gravel lot. **GPS:** N37 02.769' / W78 09.012'

*The Falls of the Nottoway provides a popular natural waterslide/swimming hole combination.*

# The Hike

The Falls of the Nottoway is one of the most surprising entries in this book. There it is in the middle of nowhere—geologically speaking—yet it's a very cool series of slides offering large pools perfect for swimming. These are no sheer falls, but then, even in the mountains, Virginia doesn't have very many of those. This place reminds me of Panther Falls in that it's a classic waterfall–swimming hole combo that is best explored in the summer when it's hot out and you want to go for a swim.

When you park in the gravel lot, the service road is off to the right. Follow it for just a few feet and look for the narrower trail that's been created by decades of people thronging the falls. You'll pass under the bridge first, then enter the woods for just a few hundred feet before you see the falls on your left.

You're not likely to have this falls to yourself if it's a warm day, but the pools are big enough that plenty of people can swim here without bothering one another.

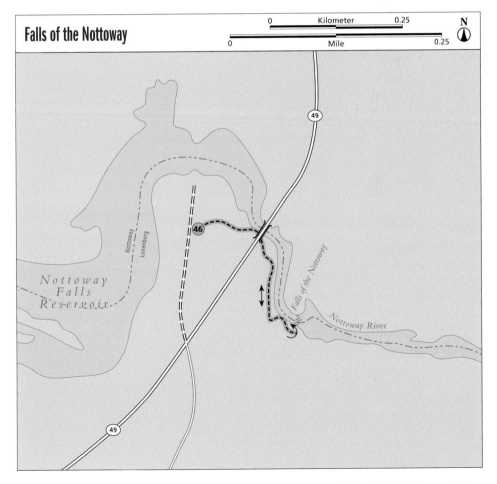

The Falls of the Nottoway is absolutely worth making a special trip for if you live in central Virginia.

## Miles and Directions

**0.0** The trail starts at the gravel service road on the right side of the parking lot. Take that about 50 feet until you see the obvious path down toward the river (under the bridge).

**0.1** Pass underneath the SR 49 bridge.

**0.2** Arrive at the falls (GPS: N37 02.666' / W78 08.908'), then retrace your steps to the trailhead.

**0.4** Arrive back at the trailhead.

# Northern Virginia

In northern Virginia, waterfall hounds will find the only "Fall Line" falls that is worthy of an entry in this book. In places like Richmond and Fredericksburg, the James and Rappahannock Rivers, respectively, flow from the Piedmont to the Costal Plain over the course of many miles. North of Washington, DC, however, the Potomac River cascades over a jumble of fractured metamorphic rocks, dropping 75 feet in less than a mile. It's quite a show the powerful Potomac puts on over that 1-mile stretch, one that's hard to peel yourself away from as you stand at the Great Falls Park overlooks.

Luckily, you don't have to go far to find the other northern Virginia entry in this book. Scott's Run Falls in a Fairfax County nature preserve is just down the road and just downstream on the Potomac from Great Falls.

Those are the only two northern Virginia cataracts that I viewed as worthy of recommending to waterfall lovers. As in the Piedmont, there are a couple of other falls that didn't make the cut. Quantico Falls lies in Prince William Forest Park. It was created by the Civilian Conservation Corps in the 1930s by blasting out an outcrop and diverting a stream. If you're planning a trip to the park, by all means check it out. The Falls on Windy Run, not far south of Scott's Run, probably rises to the level of a book-entry-quality falls immediately following a rain. Most of the time, however, there's just not enough water in the creek to warrant people going out of their way to see it. If you live in the area and want to make the trip after a deluge, you can access the falls from Windy Run Park or the Potomac Heritage Trail.

# 47 Scott's Run Falls

Just downriver from Great Falls, Scott's Run Falls drops off a granite ledge just before entering the Potomac. It's a pretty little cascade in a seemingly unlikely place. Combine it with Great Falls, and make the trip a twofer!

**Height:** 15 feet
**Start:** Two trails leave the gravel parking lot. You want the wide, gravel road, the one that heads due north toward the river.
**Distance:** 2.0 miles out and back
**Difficulty:** Easy/moderate
**Canine compatibility:** Dogs must be leashed.
**Trail surface:** Wide, gravel path
**Hiking time:** About 50 minutes

**Blaze color:** None
**County:** Fairfax
**Land status:** County park
**Trail contact:** Scott's Run Nature Preserve is managed by staff at nearby Riverbend Park, (703) 759-9018.
**Maps:** *DeLorme, Virginia Atlas and Gazetteer:* page 80, D3

**Finding the trailhead:** From I-495 west of Washington, DC, take exit 44 and head west on SR 193 (Georgetown Pike). Drive 0.2 mile on SR 193, and turn right into the first of two gravel lots for Scott's Run Nature Preserve. **GPS:** N38 57.387' / W77 11.897'

*This little-known gem, Scott's Run Falls, is downstream of Great Falls and well worth a separate trip.*

# The Hike

There are two parking lots from which you can access Scott's Run Nature Preserve. I misread the directions to this park and pulled into the one you pass first when you get off the interstate. If I had kept going down the road and parked at the second one, my 4-year-old and I would have had a shorter, flatter hike to Scott's Run Falls. Based on the map, that hike would have been about 1.2 miles round-trip.

Instead, from the first lot, we started on the wide, gravel Woodland Trail, which has a surprising amount of elevation change to it and offered a 2-mile round-trip hike. Wherever you start, you may be surprised by the beauty and size of this Fairfax County Park so close to the hustle and bustle of Washington, DC, and northern Virginia.

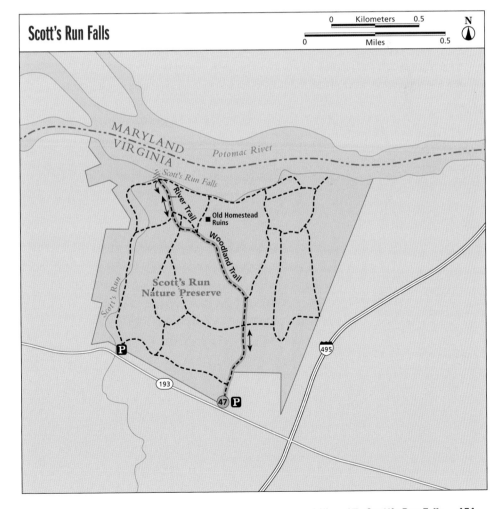

Take a look at the map before you go, and you'll see that the Woodland Trail is the one that will get you to the falls, just before Scott's Run enters the Potomac. The creek is one of many "runs" that fall steeply off the south bank of the Potomac between Roslyn and Great Falls just a few miles upstream. You cross many of them on the George Washington Parkway. Windy Run also offers a nice cascade, but it has less water in it and can't be counted on to put on a consistent show like Scott's Run Falls.

The falls also has a nice swimming hole below it, and you'll likely see people swimming in it if the weather is warm. But keep in mind that swimming is prohibited here. Not only is Scott's Run not the cleanest stream ever—its headwaters form just below the Tyson's Corner Mall—but the Potomac is very swift in this area and has currents that change constantly. Just enjoy the falls for their beauty; enjoy the hike for the serenity of the woodlands; and appreciate that a green space like this exists so close to a population center of Washington's size.

## Miles and Directions

**0.0** Take the wide gravel path—the green (on the park maps) "Woodland Trail" north.

**0.3** At the first trail junction, stay straight (somewhat left). Do not take the trail off to the right.

**0.4** At the second trail junction, go left, staying on the Woodland Trail.

**0.7** At the third trail junction (the one with the ruins of an old homestead), stay straight. Do not take the trail that goes past the ruins toward the river.

**0.8** At the fourth and final junction, you join the River Trail. Take a right onto it and walk steeply down to where Scott's Run joins the Potomac River.

**1.0** Arrive at the base of Scott's Run Falls (GPS: N38 58.064' / W77 12.135'), then retrace your steps to the trailhead.

**2.0** Arrive back at the parking lot.

# SCOTT'S RUN NATURE PRESERVE

Scott's Run Nature Preserve is notable for more than just the waterfall it contains. The Fairfax County preserve is a surprising oasis for rare and beautiful plants, including trailing arbutus, Virginia bluebells, and sessile trillium, which bloom on the park's steep hillsides. There's a grove of eastern hemlocks, which luckily haven't yet fallen victim to the hemlock woolly adelgid, and a major fault zone runs along the park's southern border.

But maybe the most intriguing thing about the park is that it exists at all, at least as something other than just another residential development along the river. According to signs in the park and information on the Fairfax County Parks website, the nature preserve grew out of a kind of citizen uprising.

In the 1960s there were 336 wooded acres along the Georgetown Pike known as the Burling Tract. The land had belonged to an attorney named Edward Burling Sr., who had a secluded cabin at the site. A developer bought the land after Burling's death in 1966 and proposed 309 cluster homes for the area that would have left about half of the site as preserved, open land.

Neighbors saw small rezoning signs in the woods, and the clash of philosophies was under way. A citizen movement to stop the development arose, and the conflict of ideas that followed over the next year eventually enveloped county residents, the governor of Virginia and local elected officials, four U. S. senators, conservation and park agencies, the federal government, the *New York Times*, a national conservation organization, developers, protesting high school students, and door-to-door petitioners.

Eventually a local public referenda passed as voters decided to tax themselves $1.5 million to purchase the land, although negotiations over the price continued. Eventually the US Department of the Interior provided $3.6 million for the purchase of the land, which today belongs to the Fairfax County Park Authority.

# 48 Great Falls

At Great Falls the Potomac River, a big, powerful river that carries a lot of water, has the steepest drop through the "Fall Line" of any eastern river.

**Height:** 40 feet

**Start:** This hike starts at the visitor center next to the main parking area.

**Distance:** 0.3 mile out and back

**Difficulty:** Easy

**Canine compatibility:** Dogs must be on a 6-foot leash.

**Trail surface:** Wide, gravel path

**Hiking time:** About 10 minutes

**Blaze color:** None

**County:** Fairfax

**Land status:** National Park

**Trail contact:** Great Falls Park, (703) 285-2965

**Maps:** *DeLorme, Virginia Atlas and Gazetteer:* page 80, D3

**Finding the trailhead:** From I-495 west of Washington, DC, take exit 44 and head west on SR 193 (Georgetown Pike). Drive 4 miles on SR 193, and turn right onto Old Dominion Drive. Drive just under a mile to the entrance to the park. Pay the $5 admission fee and drive straight ahead to the main parking area, passing the visitor center on your right. **GPS:** N38 59.828' / W77 15.283'

*The crashing power of Great Falls is a sight to behold when the Potomac is running high.*

# The Hike

At Great Falls the mighty Potomac drops about 75 feet over a distance of just under a mile. In Mather Gorge, where the true waterfalls occur, you've got maybe 40 to 50 feet of drop in a series of powerful, plunging cascades. The number of waterfalls you'll see at Great Falls varies depending on river level. In the summer, when there hasn't been a storm to fill up the watershed, there are well over a dozen distinct falls. When the river is flooding, you'll see a crashing riot of whitewater across the width of the gorge, but no single falls.

No matter when you go, the size and power of Great Falls are what strike you. And they really strike hard. Every waterfall has its own personality. Not all of them make you stand slack-jawed in wonder. Great Falls does so with the sheer scope of the scene.

My son and I observed the falls from the Virginia side. You can do so on the Maryland side as well, but these direction comments are based on our experience in

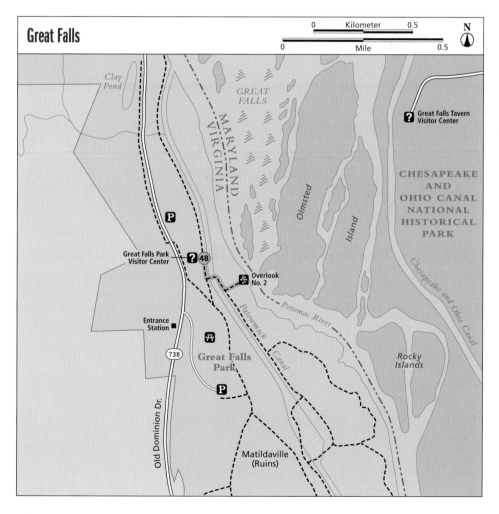

Virginia. The hike to Great Falls is a piece of cake. You park in one of the lots, locate the visitor center (you can't miss it), and follow the signs to one of three overlooks. We chose the second one. The river was moderately high on that June day, and my 4-year-old was duly impressed. If you have more time than we did that day, there are other hiking trails at the park (a unit of the National Park Service).

The River Trail gives hikers a sense idea of what the Potomac looked like before the falls and gorge formed. Hikers on that path are walking along the ancient Potomac River bed, now located 40 to 75 feet above the river's current location.

According to the National Park Service website: "Evidence of the ancient Potomac River bed can be seen in well-rounded boulders, smoothed surfaces and grooves, and beautifully formed potholes. Look for sandstone boulders along the trail, which were deposited by massive floods. The sandy soils along the river trail, with shells mixed in, are a result of sediment deposits from floods. Some of the oldest sediment deposits in the area can be found on Glade Hill, between the Matildaville and Carriage Road trails. Glade Hill was once an island in the Potomac River, and the deposits found there were left before Mather Gorge formed."

History buffs can get their fix at the visitor center. There are also horseback-riding trails and picnic tables. If you're lucky, you might see a crew of kayakers navigate the falls. Believe it or not, people really do run the Great Falls. Imagine that as you stand at an overlook marveling at the power of the place.

## Miles and Directions

**0.0**  Start on the river side of the visitor center next to the bank of porta-potties.

**0.1**  Follow the signs to the second overlook for the falls (GPS: N38 59.759' / W77 15.199').

**0.3**  Arrive back at the visitor center.

# C&O CANAL

The Great Falls hike featured in this book takes hikers to the falls from the Virginia side at the Great Falls National Park Service site. But on the other side of the river, in Potomac, Maryland, there's another National Park Service site overlooking Great Falls that's worth the time it takes to get there.

Maryland's access to Great Falls is through the Chesapeake and Ohio Canal National Historical Park. The park is actually a 183.5-mile ribbon that traces the C&O Canal and its towpath from Cumberland, Maryland, to Washington, DC. It became part of the national parks system in 1971 and now attracts 4 million visitors every year.

Where the canal passes by Great Falls, there are two overlooks, the Great Falls Tavern Visitor Center, and a number of hiking trails. If you have the time, I highly recommend the Billy Goat Trail. It's popular, so you probably won't have it to yourself, but it's a great way to explore the banks of the Potomac and includes some spectacular views of the falls. Just bear in mind that the trail is quite steep in sections and the path itself offers some rocky challenges.

The Great Falls Tavern Visitor Center—originally built in 1828—offers historical exhibits and interpretive programs. It's open daily from 9 a.m. to 4:30 p.m. And there are mule-drawn canal boat rides available to visitors from April through October.

# The Art of Hiking

When standing nose to nose with a mountain lion, you're probably not too concerned with the issue of ethical behavior in the wild. No doubt you're just terrified. But let's be honest. How often are you nose to nose with a mountain lion? For most of us, a hike into the "wild" means loading up the SUV with expensive gear and driving to a toileted trailhead. Sure, you can mourn how civilized we've become—how GPS units have replaced natural instinct and Gore-Tex stands in for true-grit—but the silly gadgets of civilization aside, we have plenty of reason to take pride in how we've matured. With survival now on the back burner, we've begun to understand that we have a responsibility to protect, no longer just conquer, our wild places: that they, not we, are at risk. So please, do what you can. The following section will help you understand better what it means to "do what you can" while still making the most of your hiking experience. Anyone can take a hike, but hiking safely and well is an art requiring preparation and proper equipment.

## Trail Etiquette

**Leave no trace.** Always leave an area just like you found it—if not better than you found it. Avoid camping in fragile, alpine meadows and along the banks of streams and lakes. Use a camp stove versus building a wood fire. Pack up all of your trash and extra food. Bury human waste at least 100 feet from water sources under 6 to 8 inches of topsoil. Don't bathe with soap in a lake or stream—use prepackaged moistened towels to wipe off sweat and dirt, or bathe in the water without soap.

**Stay on the trail.** It's true, a path anywhere leads nowhere new, but purists will just have to get over it. Paths serve an important purpose; they limit impact on natural areas. Straying from a designated trail may seem innocent but it can cause damage to sensitive areas—damage that may take years to recover, if it can recover at all. Even simple shortcuts can be destructive. So, please, stay on the trail.

**Leave no weeds.** Noxious weeds tend to overtake other plants, which in turn affects animals and birds that depend on them for food. To minimize the spread of noxious weeds, hikers should regularly clean their boots, tents, packs, and hiking poles of mud and seeds. Also brush your dog to remove any weed seeds before heading off into a new area.

**Keep your dog under control.** You can buy a flexi-lead that allows your dog to go exploring along the trail, while allowing you the ability to reel him in should another hiker approach or should he decide to chase a rabbit. Always obey leash laws and be sure to bury your dog's waste or pack it in resealable plastic bags.

**Respect other trail users.** Often you're not the only one on the trail. With the rise in popularity of multiuse trails, you'll have to learn a new kind of respect, beyond the nod and "hello" approach you may be used to. First investigate whether you're on a multiuse trail, and assume the appropriate precautions. When you encounter motorized vehicles (ATVs, motorcycles, and 4WDs), be alert. Though they should always yield to the hiker, often they're going too fast or are too lost in the buzz of their engine to react to your presence. If you hear activity ahead, step off the trail just to be safe. Note that you're not likely to hear a mountain biker coming, so be prepared and know ahead of time whether you share the trail with them. Cyclists should always yield to hikers, but that's little comfort to the hiker. Be aware. When you approach horses or pack animals on the trail, always step quietly off the trail, preferably on the downhill side, and let them pass. If you're wearing a large backpack, it's often a good idea to sit down. To some animals, a hiker wearing a large backpack might appear threatening. Many national forests allow domesticated grazing, usually for sheep and cattle. Make sure your dog doesn't harass these animals, and respect ranchers' rights while you're enjoying yours.

## Getting into Shape

Unless you want to be sore—and possibly have to shorten your trip or vacation—be sure to get in shape before a big hike. If you're terribly out of shape, start a walking program early, preferably eight weeks in advance. Start with a 15-minute walk during your lunch hour or after work and gradually increase your walking time to an hour. You should also increase your elevation gain. Walking briskly up hills really strengthens your leg muscles and gets your heart rate up. If you work in a storied office building, take the stairs instead of the elevator. If you prefer going to a gym, walk the treadmill or use a stair machine. You can further increase your strength and endurance by walking with a loaded backpack. Stationary exercises you might consider are squats, leg lifts, sit-ups, and push-ups. Other good ways to get in shape include biking, running, aerobics, and, of course, short hikes. Stretching before and after a hike keeps muscles flexible and helps avoid injuries.

## Preparedness

It's been said that failing to plan means planning to fail. So do take the necessary time to plan your trip. Whether going on a short day hike or an extended backpack trip, always prepare for the worst. Simply remembering to pack a copy of the *U.S. Army Survival Manual* is not preparedness. Although it's not a bad idea if you plan on entering truly wild places, it's merely the tourniquet answer to a problem. You need to do your best to prevent the problem from arising in the first place. In order to survive—and to stay reasonably comfortable—you need to concern yourself with the basics: water, food, and shelter. Don't go on a hike without having these bases covered. And don't go on a hike expecting to find these items in the woods.

**Water.** Even in frigid conditions, you need at least two quarts of water a day to function efficiently. Add heat and taxing terrain and you can bump that figure up to one gallon. That's simply a base to work from—your metabolism and your level of conditioning can raise or lower that amount. Unless you know your level, assume that you need one gallon of water a day. Now, where do you plan on getting the water?

Preferably not from natural water sources. These sources can be loaded with intestinal disturbers, such as bacteria, viruses, and fertilizers. *Giardia lamblia,* the most common of these disturbers, is a protozoan parasite that lives part of its life cycle as a cyst in water sources. The parasite spreads when mammals defecate in water sources. Once ingested, Giardia can induce cramping, diarrhea, vomiting, and fatigue within two days to two weeks after ingestion. Giardiasis is treatable with prescription drugs. If you believe you've contracted giardiasis, see a doctor immediately.

**Treating water.** The best and easiest solution to avoid polluted water is to carry your water with you. Yet, depending on the nature of your hike and the duration, this may not be an option—one gallon of water weighs eight-and-a-half pounds. In that case you'll need to look into treating water. Regardless of which method you choose, you should always carry some water with you in case of an emergency. Save this reserve until you absolutely need it.

There are three methods of treating water: boiling, chemical treatment, and filtering. If you boil water, it's recommended that you do so for 10 to 15 minutes. This is often impractical because you're forced to exhaust a great deal of your fuel supply. You can opt for chemical treatment, which will kill Giardia but will not take care of other chemical pollutants. Another drawback to chemical treatments is the unpleasant taste of the water after it's treated. You can remedy this by adding powdered drink mix to the water. Filters are the preferred method for treating water. Many filters remove Giardia, organic and inorganic contaminants, and don't leave an aftertaste. Water filters are far from perfect as they can easily become clogged or leak if a gasket wears out. It's always a good idea to carry a backup supply of chemical treatment tablets in case your filter decides to quit on you.

**Food.** If we're talking about survival, you can go days without food, as long as you have water. But we're also talking about comfort. Try to avoid foods that are high in sugar and fat like candy bars and potato chips. These food types are harder to digest and are low in nutritional value. Instead, bring along foods that are easy to pack, nutritious, and high in energy (e.g., bagels, nutrition bars, dehydrated fruit, gorp, and jerky). If you are on an overnight trip, easy-to-fix dinners include rice mixes with dehydrated potatoes, corn, pasta with cheese sauce, and soup mixes. For a tasty breakfast, you can fix hot oatmeal with brown sugar and reconstituted milk powder topped off with banana chips. If you like a hot drink in the morning, bring along herbal tea bags or hot chocolate. If you are a coffee junkie, you can purchase coffee that is packaged like tea bags. You can prepackage all of your meals in heavy-duty resealable plastic bags to keep food from spilling in your pack. These bags can be reused to pack out trash.

**Shelter.** The type of shelter you choose depends less on the conditions than on your tolerance for discomfort. Shelter comes in many forms—tent, tarp, lean-to, bivy sack, cabin, cave, etc. If you're camping in the desert, a bivy sack may suffice, but if you're above the treeline and a storm is approaching, a better choice is a three- or four-season tent. Tents are the logical and most popular choice for most backpackers as they're lightweight and packable—and you can rest assured that you always have shelter from the elements. Before you leave on your trip, anticipate what the weather and terrain will be like and plan for the type of shelter that will work best for your comfort level (see Equipment later in this section).

**Finding a campsite.** If there are established campsites, stick to those. If not, start looking for a campsite early—around 3:30 or 4:00 P.M. Stop at the first decent site you see. Depending on the area, it could be a long time before you find another suitable location. Pitch your camp in an area that's level. Make sure the area is at least 200 feet from fragile areas like lakeshores, meadows, and stream banks. And try to avoid areas thick in underbrush, as they can harbor insects and provide cover for approaching animals.

If you are camping in stormy, rainy weather, look for a rock outcrop or a shelter in the trees to keep the wind from blowing your tent all night. Be sure that you don't camp under trees with dead limbs that might break off on top of you. Also, try to find an area that has an absorbent surface, such as sandy soil or forest duff. This, in addition to camping on a surface with a slight angle, will provide better drainage. By all means, don't dig trenches to provide drainage around your tent—remember you're practicing zero-impact camping.

If you're in bear country, steer clear of creekbeds or animal paths. If you see any signs of a bear's presence (i.e., scat, footprints), relocate. You'll need to find a campsite near a tall tree where you can hang your food and other items that may attract bears such as deodorant, toothpaste, or soap. Carry a lightweight nylon rope with which to hang your food. As a rule, you should hang your food at least 20 feet from the ground and 5 feet away from the tree trunk. You can put food and other items in a waterproof stuff sack and tie one end of the rope to the stuff sack. To get the other end of the rope over the tree branch, tie a good size rock to it, and gently toss the rock over the tree branch. Pull the stuff sack up until it reaches the top of the branch and tie it off securely. Don't hang your food near your tent! If possible, hang your food at least 100 feet away from your campsite. Alternatives to hanging your food are bear-proof plastic tubes and metal bear boxes.

Lastly, think of comfort. Lie down on the ground where you intend to sleep and see if it's a good fit. For morning warmth (and a nice view to wake up to), have your tent face east.

## First Aid

I know you're tough, but get 10 miles into the woods and develop a blister and you'll wish you had carried that first-aid kit. Face it: it's just plain good sense. Many companies produce lightweight, compact first-aid kits. Just make sure yours contains at least the following:

❑ Ace bandage                    ❑ antibacterial wipes

❑ adhesive bandages              ❑ antihistamine

❑ antacid tablets                ❑ aspirin

- ❑ Betadine solution
- ❑ first-aid book
- ❑ moleskin or duct tape
- ❑ plastic gloves
- ❑ scissors
- ❑ sterile cotton tip applicators
- ❑ sterile gauze and dressings
- ❑ surgical tape
- ❑ syrup of ipecac (to induce vomiting)
- ❑ thermometer
- ❑ triple-antibiotic ointment
- ❑ tweezers
- ❑ wire splint

Here are a few tips for dealing with and hopefully preventing certain ailments.

**Sunburn.** Take along sunscreen or sun block, protective clothing, and a wide-brimmed hat. If you do get a sunburn, treat the area with aloe vera gel, and protect the area from further sun exposure. At higher elevations the sun's radiation can be particularly damaging to skin. Remember that your eyes are vulnerable to this radiation as well. Sunglasses can be a good way to prevent headaches and permanent eye damage from the sun, especially in places where light-colored rock or patches of snow reflect light up in your face.

**Blisters.** Be prepared to take care of these hike-spoilers by carrying moleskin (a lightly padded adhesive), gauze and tape, or adhesive bandages. An effective way to apply moleskin is to cut out a circle of moleskin and remove the center—like a doughnut—and place it over the blistered area. Cutting the center out will reduce the pressure applied to the sensitive skin. Other products can help you combat blisters. Some are applied to suspicious hot spots before a blister forms to help decrease friction to that area, while others are applied to the blister after it has popped to help prevent further irritation.

**Insect bites and stings.** You can treat most insect bites and stings by applying hydrocortisone 1% cream topically and taking a pain medication such as ibuprofen or acetaminophen to reduce swelling. If you forgot to pack these items, a cold compress or a paste of mud and ashes can sometimes assuage the itching and discomfort. Remove any stingers by using tweezers or scraping the area with your fingernail or a knife blade. Don't pinch the area as you'll only spread the venom.

Some hikers are highly sensitive to bites and stings and may have a serious allergic reaction that can be life threatening. Symptoms of a serious allergic reaction can include wheezing, an asthmatic attack, and shock. The treatment for this severe type of reaction is epinephrine. If you know that you are sensitive to bites and stings, carry a pre-packaged kit of epinephrine, which can be obtained only by prescription from your doctor.

**Ticks.** Ticks can carry diseases such as Rocky Mountain spotted fever and Lyme disease. The best defense is, of course, prevention. If you know you're going to be hiking through an area littered with ticks, wear long pants and a long-sleeved shirt. You can apply a permethrin repellent to your clothing and a DEET repellent to exposed skin. At the end of your hike, do a spot check for ticks (and insects in general). If you do find a tick, grab the head of the tick firmly—with a pair of tweezers if you have them—and gently pull it away from the skin with a twisting motion. Sometimes the mouth parts linger, embedded in your skin. If this happens, try to remove them with a disinfected needle. Clean the affected area with an antibacterial cleanser and then apply triple antibiotic ointment. Monitor the area for a few days. If irritation persists or a white spot develops, see a doctor for possible infection.

**Poison ivy, oak, and sumac.** These skin irritants can be found most anywhere in North America and come in the form of a bush or a vine, having leaflets in groups of three, five, seven, or nine. Learn how to spot the plants. The oil they secrete can cause an allergic reaction in the form of blisters, usually about 12 hours after exposure. The itchy rash can last from ten days to several weeks. The best defense against these irritants is to wear clothing that covers the arms, legs and torso. For summer, zip-off cargo pants come in handy. There are also nonprescription lotions you can apply to exposed skin that guard against the effects of poison ivy/oak/sumac and can be washed off with soap and water. If you think you were in contact with the plants, after hiking (or even on the trail during longer hikes) wash with soap and water. Taking a hot shower with soap after you return home from your hike will also help to remove any lingering oil from your skin. Should you contract a rash from any of these plants, use an antihistamine to reduce the itching. If the rash is localized, create a light bleach/water wash to dry up the area. If the rash has spread, either tough it out or see your doctor about getting a dose of cortisone (available both orally and by injection).

**Snakebites.** Snakebites are rare in North America. Unless startled or provoked, the majority of snakes will not bite. If you are wise to their habitats and keep a careful eye on the trail, you should be just fine. When stepping over logs, first step on the log, making sure you can see what's on the other side before stepping down. Though your chances of being struck are slim, it's wise to know what to do in the event you are.

If a *nonpoisonous* snake bites you, allow the wound to bleed a small amount and then cleanse the wounded area with a Betadine solution (10% povidone iodine). Rinse the wound with clean water (preferably) or fresh urine (it might sound ugly, but it's sterile). Once the area is clean, cover it with triple antibiotic ointment and a clean bandage. Remember, most residual damage from snakebites, poisonous or otherwise, comes from infection, not the snake's venom. Keep the area as clean as possible and get medical attention immediately.

If somebody in your party is bitten by a poisonous snake, follow these steps:
1. Calm the patient.
2. Remove jewelry, watches, and restrictive clothing, and immobilize the affected limb. Do not elevate the injury. Medical opinions vary on whether the area should be lower or level with the heart, but the consensus is that it should not be above it.
3. Make a note of the circumference of the limb at the bite site and at various points above the site as well. This will help you monitor swelling.

4. Evacuate your victim. Ideally he should be carried out to minimize movement. If the victim appears to be doing okay, he can walk. Stop and rest frequently, and if the swelling appears to be spreading or the patient's symptoms increase, change your plan and find a way to get your patient transported.

5. If you are waiting for rescue, make sure to keep your patient comfortable and hydrated (unless he begins vomiting).

Snakebite treatment is rife with old-fashioned remedies: You used to be told to cut and suck the venom out of the bite site or to use a suction cup extractor for the same purpose; applying an electric shock to the area was even in vogue for a while. Do not do any of these things. Do not apply ice, do not give your patient painkillers, and do not apply a tourniquet. All you really want to do is keep your patient calm and get help. If you're alone and have to hike out, don't run—you'll only increase the flow of blood throughout your system. Instead, walk calmly.

**Dehydration.** Have you ever hiked in hot weather and had a roaring headache and felt fatigued after only a few miles? More than likely you were dehydrated. Symptoms of dehydration include fatigue, headache, and decreased coordination and judgment. When you are hiking, your body's rate of fluid loss depends on the outside temperature, humidity, altitude, and your activity level. On average a hiker walking in warm weather will lose four liters of fluid a day. That fluid loss is easily replaced by normal consumption of liquids and food. However, if a hiker is walking briskly in hot, dry weather and hauling a heavy pack, he or she can lose one to three liters of water an hour. It's important to always carry plenty of water and to stop often and drink fluids regularly, even if you aren't thirsty.

**Heat exhaustion** is the result of a loss of large amounts of electrolytes and often occurs if a hiker is dehydrated and has been under heavy exertion. Common symptoms of heat exhaustion include cramping, exhaustion, fatigue, lightheadedness, and nausea. You can treat heat exhaustion by getting out of the sun and drinking an electrolyte solution made up of one teaspoon of salt and one tablespoon of sugar dissolved in a liter of water. Drink this solution slowly over a period of 1 hour. Drinking plenty of fluids (preferably an electrolyte solution/sports drink) can prevent heat exhaustion. Avoid hiking during the hottest parts of the day, and wear breathable clothing, a wide-brimmed hat, and sunglasses.

**Hypothermia** is one of the biggest dangers in the backcountry, especially for day hikers in the summertime. That may sound strange, but imagine starting out on a hike in midsummer when it's sunny and 80°F out. You're clad in nylon shorts and a cotton T-shirt. About halfway through your hike, the sky begins to cloud up, and in the next hour a light drizzle begins to fall and the wind starts to pick up. Before you know it, you are soaking wet and shivering—the perfect recipe for hypothermia. More advanced signs include decreased coordination, slurred speech, and blurred vision. When a victim's temperature falls below 92°F, the blood pressure and pulse plummet, possibly leading to coma and death.

To avoid hypothermia, always bring a windproof/rainproof shell, a fleece jacket, long underwear made of a breathable, synthetic fiber, gloves, and hat when you are hiking in the mountains. Learn to adjust your clothing layers based on the temperature. If you are climbing uphill at a moderate pace you will stay warm, but when you stop for a break you'll become cold quickly, unless you add more layers of clothing.

If a hiker is showing advanced signs of hypothermia, dress him or her in dry clothes and make sure he or she is wearing a hat and gloves. Place the person in a sleeping bag in a tent or shelter that will protect him or her from the wind and other elements. Give the person warm fluids to drink and keep him awake.

**Frostbite.** When the mercury dips below 32°F, your extremities begin to chill. If a persistent chill attacks a localized area, say, your hands or your toes, the circulatory system reacts by cutting off blood flow to the affected area—the idea being to protect and preserve the body's overall temperature. And so it's death by attrition for the affected area. Ice crystals start to form from the water in the cells of the neglected tissue. Deprived of heat, nourishment, and now water, the tissue literally starves. This is frostbite.

Prevention is your best defense against this situation. Most prone to frostbite are your face, hands, and feet, so protect these areas well. Wool is the traditional material of choice because it provides ample air space for insulation and draws moisture away from the skin. Synthetic fabrics, however, have made great strides in the cold weather clothing market. Do your research. A pair of light silk liners under your regular gloves is a good trick for keeping warm. They afford some additional warmth, but more importantly they'll allow you to remove your mitts for tedious work without exposing the skin.

If your feet or hands start to feel cold or numb due to the elements, warm them as quickly as possible. Place cold hands under your armpits or bury them in your crotch. If your feet are cold, change your socks. If there's plenty of room in your boots, add another pair of socks. Do remember, though, that constricting your feet in tight boots can restrict blood flow and actually make your feet colder more quickly. Your socks need to have breathing room if they're going to be effective. Dead air provides insulation. If your face is cold, place your warm hands over your face, or simply wear a head stocking.

Should your skin go numb and start to appear white and waxy, chances are you've got or are developing frostbite. Don't try to thaw the area unless you can maintain the warmth. In other words, don't stop to warm up your frostbitten feet only to head back on the trail. You'll do more damage than good. Tests have shown that hikers who walked on thawed feet did more harm, and endured more pain, than hikers who left the affected areas alone. Do your best to get out of the cold entirely and seek medical attention—which usually consists of performing a rapid rewarming in water for 20 to 30 minutes.

The overall objective in preventing both hypothermia and frostbite is to keep the body's core warm. Protect key areas where heat escapes, like the top of the head, and maintain the proper nutrition level. Foods that are high in calories aid the body in producing heat. Never smoke or drink when you're in situations where the cold is threatening. By affecting blood flow, these activities ultimately cool the body's core temperature.

**Altitude sickness (AMS).** High lofty peaks, clear alpine lakes, and vast mountain views beckon hikers to the high country. But those who like to venture high may become victims of altitude sickness (also known as Acute Mountain Sickness—AMS). Altitude sickness is your body's reaction to insufficient oxygen in the blood due to decreased barometric pressure. While some hikers may feel lightheaded, nauseous, and experience shortness of breath at 7,000 feet, others may not experience these symptoms until they reach 10,000 feet or higher.

Slowing your ascent to high places and giving your body a chance to acclimatize to the higher elevations can prevent altitude sickness. For example, if you live at sea level and are planning a weeklong backpacking trip to elevations between 7,000 and 12,000 feet, start by staying below 7,000 feet for one night, then move to between 7,000 and 10,000 feet for another night or two. Avoid strenuous exertion and alcohol to give your body a chance to adjust to the new altitude. It's also important to eat light food and drink plenty of nonalcoholic fluids, preferably water. Loss of appetite at altitude is common, but you must eat!

Most hikers who experience mild to moderate AMS develop a headache and/or nausea, grow lethargic, and have problems sleeping. The treatment for AMS is simple: stop heading uphill. Keep eating and drinking water and take meds for the headache. You actually need to take more breaths at altitude than at sea level, so breathe a little faster without hyperventilating. If symptoms don't improve over 24 to 48 hours, descend. Once a victim descends about 2,000 to 3,000 feet, his signs will usually begin to diminish.

Severe AMS comes in two forms: High Altitude Pulmonary Edema (HAPE) and High Altitude Cerebral Edema (HACE). HAPE, an accumulation of fluid in the lungs, can occur above 8,000 feet. Symptoms include rapid heart rate, shortness of breath at rest, AMS symptoms, dry cough developing into a wet cough, gurgling sounds, flu-like or bronchitis symptoms, and lack of muscle coordination. HAPE is life threatening so descend immediately, at least 2,000 to 4,000 feet. HACE usually occurs above 12,000 feet but sometimes occurs above 10,000 feet. Symptoms are similar to HAPE but also include seizures, hallucinations, paralysis, and vision disturbances. Descend immediately—HACE is also life threatening.

**Hantavirus Pulmonary Syndrome (HPS).** Deer mice spread the virus that causes HPS, and humans contract it from breathing it in, usually when they've disturbed an area with dust and mice feces from nests or surfaces with mice droppings or urine. Exposure to large numbers of rodents and their feces or urine presents the greatest risk. As hikers, we sometimes enter old buildings, and often deer mice live in these places. We may not be around long enough to be exposed, but do be aware of this disease. About half the people who develop HPS die. Symptoms are flu-like and appear about two to three weeks after exposure. After initial symptoms, a dry cough and shortness of breath follow. Breathing is difficult. If you even think you might have HPS, see a doctor immediately!

## Natural Hazards

Besides tripping over a rock or tree root on the trail, there are some real hazards to be aware of while hiking. Even if where you're hiking doesn't have the plethora of poisonous snakes and plants, insects, and grizzly bears found in other parts of the United States, there are a few weather conditions and predators you may need to take into account.

**Lightning.** Thunderstorms build over the mountains almost every day during the summer. Lightning is generated by thunderheads and can strike without warning, even several miles away from the nearest overhead cloud. The best rule of thumb is to start leaving exposed peaks, ridges, and canyon rims by about noon. This time can vary a little depending on storm buildup. Keep an eye on cloud formation and don't underestimate how fast a storm can build. The bigger they get, the more likely a thunderstorm will happen. Lightning takes the path of least resistance, so if you're the high point, it might choose you. Ducking under a rock overhang is dangerous as you form the shortest path between the rock and ground. If you dash below treeline, avoid standing under the only or the tallest tree. If you are caught above treeline, stay away from anything metal you might be carrying, Move down off the ridge slightly to a low, treeless point and squat until the storm passes. If you have an insulating pad, squat on it. Avoid having both your hands and feet touching the ground at once and never lie flat. If you hear a buzzing sound or feel your hair standing on end, move quickly as an electrical charge is building up.

**Flash floods.** On July 31, 1976, a torrential downpour unleashed by a thunderstorm dumped tons of water into the Big Thompson watershed near Estes Park. Within hours, a wall of water moved down the narrow canyon killing 139 people and causing more than $30 million in property damage. The spooky thing about flash floods, especially in western canyons, is that they can appear out of nowhere from a storm many miles away. While hiking or driving in canyons, keep an eye on the weather. Always climb to safety if danger threatens. Flash floods usually subside quickly, so be patient and don't cross a swollen stream.

**Bears.** Most of the United States (outside of the Pacific Northwest and parts of the Northern Rockies) does not have a grizzly bear population, although some rumors exist about sightings where there should be none. Black bears are plentiful, however. Here are some tips in case you and a bear scare each other. Most of all, avoid surprising a bear. Talk or sing where visibility or hearing are limited, such as along a rushing creek or in thick brush. In grizzly country especially, carry bear spray in a holster on your pack belt where you can quickly grab it. While hiking, watch for bear tracks (five toes), droppings (sizable with leaves, partly digested berries, seeds, and/or animal fur), or rocks and roots along the trail that show signs of being dug up (this could be a bear looking for bugs to eat). Keep a clean camp, hang food or use bearproof storage containers, and don't sleep in the clothes you wore while cooking. Be especially careful to avoid getting between a mother and her cubs. In late summer and fall bears are busy eating to fatten up for winter, so be extra careful around berry bushes and oakbrush. If you do encounter a bear, move away slowly while facing the bear, talk softly, and avoid direct eye contact. Give the bear room to escape. Since bears are very curious, it might stand upright to get a better whiff of you, and it may even charge you to try to intimidate you. Try to stay calm. If a black bear attacks you, fight back with anything you have handy. If a grizzly bear attacks you, your best option is to "play dead" by lying face down on the ground and covering the back of your neck and head with your hands. Unleashed dogs have been known to come running back to their owners with a bear close behind. Keep your dog on a leash or leave it at home.

**Mountain lions.** Mountain lions appear to be getting more comfortable around humans as long as deer (their favorite prey) are in an area with adequate cover. Usually elusive and quiet, lions rarely attack people. If you meet a lion, give it a chance to escape. Stay calm and talk firmly to it. Back away slowly while facing the lion. If you run, you'll only encourage the cat to chase you. Make yourself look large by opening a jacket, if you have one, or waving your hiking poles. If the lion behaves aggressively throw stones, sticks, or whatever you can while remaining tall. If a lion does attack, fight for your life with anything you can grab.

**Moose.** Because moose have very few natural predators, they don't fear humans like other animals. You might find moose in sagebrush and wetter areas of willow, aspen, and pine, or in beaver habitats. Mothers with calves, as well as bulls during mating season, can be particularly aggressive. If a moose threatens you, back away slowly and talk calmly to it. Keep your pets away from moose.

**Other considerations.** Hunting is a popular sport in the United States, especially during rifle season in October and November. Hiking is still enjoyable in those months in many areas, so just take a few precautions. First, learn when the different hunting seasons start and end in the area in which you'll be hiking. During this time frame, be sure to wear at least a blaze orange hat, and possibly put an orange vest over your pack. Don't be surprised to see hunters in camo outfits carrying bows or rifles around during their season. If you would feel more comfortable without hunters around, hike in national parks and monuments or state and local parks where hunting is not allowed.

### Navigation

Whether you are going on a short hike in a familiar area or planning a weeklong backpack trip, you should always be equipped with the proper navigational equipment—at the very least a detailed map and a sturdy compass.

**Maps.** There are many different types of maps available to help you find your way on the trail. Easiest to find are Forest Service maps and BLM (Bureau of Land

Management) maps. These maps tend to cover large areas, so be sure they are detailed enough for your particular trip. You can also obtain National Park maps as well as high quality maps from private companies and trail groups. These maps can be obtained either from outdoor stores or ranger stations.

U.S. Geological Survey topographic maps are particularly popular with hikers—especially serious backcountry hikers. These maps contain the standard map symbols such as roads, lakes, and rivers, as well as contour lines that show the details of the trail terrain like ridges, valleys, passes, and mountain peaks. The 7.5-minute series (1 inch on the map equals approximately 0.4 mile on the ground) provides the closest inspection available. USGS maps are available by mail (U.S. Geological Survey, Map Distribution Branch, PO Box 25286, Denver, CO 80225), or at mapping.usgs.gov/esic/to_order.html.

If you want to check out the high-tech world of maps, you can purchase topographic maps on CD-ROM. These software-mapping programs let you select a route on your computer, print it out, then take it with you on the trail. Some software mapping programs let you insert symbols and labels, download waypoints from a GPS unit, and export the maps to other software programs.

The art of map reading is a skill that you can develop by first practicing in an area you are familiar with. To begin, orient the map so the map is lined up in the correct direction (i.e., north on the map is lined up with true north). Next, familiarize yourself with the map symbols and try and match them up with terrain features around you such as a high ridge, mountain peak, river, or lake. If you are practicing with a USGS map, notice the contour lines. On gentler terrain these contour lines are spaced farther apart, and on steeper terrain they are closer together. Pick a short loop trail, and stop frequently to check your position on the map. As you practice map reading, you'll learn how to anticipate a steep section on the trail or a good place to take a rest break, and so on.

**Compasses.** First off, the sun is not a substitute for a compass. So, what kind of compass should you have? Here are some characteristics you should look for: a rectangular base with detailed scales, a liquid-filled housing, protective housing, a sighting line on the mirror, luminous alignment and back-bearing arrows, a luminous north-seeking arrow, and a well-defined bezel ring.

You can learn compass basics by reading the detailed instructions included with your compass. If you want to fine-tune your compass skills, sign up for an orienteering class or purchase a book on compass reading. Once you've learned the basic skills of using a compass, remember to practice these skills before you head into the backcountry.

If you are a klutz at using a compass, you may be interested in checking out the technical wizardry of the GPS (Global Positioning System) device. The GPS was developed by the Pentagon and works off twenty-four NAVSTAR satellites, which were designed to guide missiles to their targets. A GPS device is a handheld unit that calculates your latitude and longitude with the easy press of a button. The Department of Defense used to scramble the satellite signals a bit to prevent civilians (and spies!)

from getting extremely accurate readings, but that practice was discontinued in May 2000, and GPS units now provide nearly pinpoint accuracy (within 30 to 60 feet).

There are many different types of GPS units available, and they range in price from $100 to $400. In general, all GPS units have a display screen and keypad where you input information. In addition to acting as a compass, the unit allows you to plot your route, easily retrace your path, track your travelling speed, find the mileage between waypoints, and calculate the total mileage of your route.

Before you purchase a GPS unit, keep in mind that these devices don't pick up signals indoors, in heavily wooded areas, on mountain peaks, or in deep valleys. Also, batteries can wear out or other technical problems can develop. A GPS unit should be used in conjunction with a map and compass, not in place of those items.

**Pedometers.** A pedometer is a small, clip-on unit with a digital display that calculates your hiking distance in miles or kilometers based on your walking stride. Some units also calculate the calories you burn and your total hiking time. Pedometers are available at most large outdoor stores and range in price from $20 to $40.

## Trip Planning

Planning your hiking adventure begins with letting a friend or relative know your trip itinerary so they can call for help if you don't return at your scheduled time. Your next task is to make sure you are outfitted to experience the risks and rewards of the trail. This section highlights gear and clothing you may want to take with you to get the most out of your hike.

### Day Hike

❑ bear repellent spray (if hiking in grizzly country)
❑ camera
❑ compass/GPS unit
❑ pedometer
❑ daypack
❑ first-aid kit
❑ food
❑ guidebook
❑ headlamp/flashlight with extra batteries and bulbs
❑ hat
❑ insect repellent

❑ knife/multipurpose tool
❑ map
❑ matches in waterproof container and fire starter
❑ fleece jacket
❑ rain gear
❑ space blanket
❑ sunglasses
❑ sunscreen
❑ swimsuit and/or fishing gear (if hiking to a lake)
❑ watch
❑ water
❑ water bottles/water hydration system

### Overnight Trip

❑ backpack and waterproof rain cover

❑ backpacker's trowel

- ❏ bandanna
- ❏ bear repellent spray (if hiking in grizzly country)
- ❏ bear bell
- ❏ biodegradable soap
- ❏ pot scrubber
- ❏ collapsible water container (2–3 gallon capacity)
- ❏ clothing—extra wool socks, shirt, and shorts
- ❏ cook set/utensils
- ❏ ditty bags to store gear
- ❏ extra plastic resealable bags
- ❏ gaiters
- ❏ garbage bag
- ❏ ground cloth
- ❏ journal/pen
- ❏ nylon rope to hang food
- ❏ long underwear
- ❏ permit (if required)
- ❏ rain jacket and pants
- ❏ sandals to wear around camp and to ford streams
- ❏ sleeping bag
- ❏ waterproof stuff sack
- ❏ sleeping pad
- ❏ small bath towel
- ❏ stove and fuel
- ❏ tent
- ❏ toiletry items
- ❏ water filter
- ❏ whistle

## Equipment

With the outdoor market currently flooded with products, many of which are pure gimmickry, it seems impossible to both differentiate and choose. Do I really need a tropical-fish-lined collapsible shower? (No, you don't.) The only defense against the maddening quantity of items thrust in your face is to think practically—and to do so before you go shopping. The worst buys are impulsive buys. Since most name brands will differ only slightly in quality, it's best to know what you're looking for in terms of function. Buy only what you need. You will, don't forget, be carrying what you've bought on your back. Here are some things to keep in mind before you go shopping.

**Clothes.** Clothing is your armor against Mother Nature's little surprises. Hikers should be prepared for any possibility, especially when hiking in mountainous areas. Adequate rain protection and extra layers of clothing are a good idea. In summer, a wide-brimmed hat can help keep the sun at bay. In the winter months the first layer you'll want to wear is a "wicking" layer of long underwear that keeps perspiration away from your skin. Wear long underwear made from synthetic fibers that wick moisture away from the skin and draw it toward the next layer of clothing, where it then evaporates. Avoid wearing long underwear made of cotton as it is slow to dry and keeps moisture next to your skin.

The second layer you'll wear is the "insulating" layer. Aside from keeping you warm, this layer needs to "breathe" so you stay dry while hiking. A fabric that provides insulation and dries quickly is fleece. It's interesting to note that this one-of-a-kind fabric is made out of recycled plastic. Purchasing a zip-up jacket made of this material is highly recommended.

The last line of layering defense is the "shell" layer. You'll need some type of waterproof, windproof, breathable jacket that will fit over all of your other layers. It should have a large hood that fits over a hat. You'll also need a good pair of rain pants made from a similar waterproof, breathable fabric. Some Gore-Tex jackets cost as much as $500, but you should know that there are more affordable fabrics out there that work just as well.

Now that you've learned the basics of layering, you can't forget to protect your hands and face. In cold, windy, or rainy weather you'll need a hat made of wool or fleece and insulated, waterproof gloves that will keep your hands warm and toasty. As mentioned earlier, buying an additional pair of light silk liners to wear under your regular gloves is a good idea.

**Footwear.** If you have any extra money to spend on your trip, put that money into boots or trail shoes. Poor shoes will bring a hike to a halt faster than anything else. To avoid this annoyance, buy shoes that provide support and are lightweight and flexible. A lightweight hiking boot is better than a heavy, leather mountaineering boot for most day hikes and backpacking. Trail running shoes provide a little extra cushion and are made in a high-top style that many people wear for hiking. These running shoes are lighter, more flexible, and more breathable than hiking boots. If you know you'll be hiking in wet weather often, purchase boots or shoes with a Gore-Tex liner, which will help keep your feet dry.

When buying your boots, be sure to wear the same type of socks you'll be wearing on the trail. If the boots you're buying are for cold weather hiking, try the boots on while wearing two pairs of socks. Speaking of socks, a good cold weather sock combination is to wear a thinner sock made of wool or polypropylene covered by a heavier outer sock made of wool or a synthetic/wool mix. The inner sock protects the foot from the rubbing effects of the outer sock and prevents blisters. Many outdoor stores have some type of ramp to simulate hiking uphill and downhill. Be sure to take advantage of this test, as toe-jamming boot fronts can be very painful and debilitating on the downhill trek.

Once you've purchased your footwear, be sure to break them in before you hit the trail. New footwear is often stiff and needs to be stretched and molded to your foot.

**Hiking poles.** Hiking poles help with balance, and more importantly take pressure off your knees. The ones with shock absorbers are easier on your elbows and knees. Some poles even come with a camera attachment to be used as a monopod. And heaven forbid you meet a mountain lion, bear, or unfriendly dog, the poles can make you look a lot bigger.

**Backpacks.** No matter what type of hiking you do you'll need a pack of some sort to carry the basic trail essentials. There are a variety of backpacks on the market, but let's first discuss what you intend to use it for. Day hikes or overnight trips?

If you plan on doing a day hike, a daypack should have some of the following characteristics: a padded hip belt that's at least 2 inches in diameter (avoid packs with only a small nylon piece of webbing for a hip belt); a chest strap (the chest strap helps stabilize the pack against your body); external pockets to carry water and other items that you want easy access to; an internal pocket to hold keys, a knife, a wallet, and other miscellaneous items; an external lashing system to hold a jacket; and, if you so desire, a hydration pocket for carrying a hydration system (which consists of a water bladder with an attachable drinking hose).

For short hikes, some hikers like to use a fanny pack to store just a camera, food, a compass, a map, and other trail essentials. Most fanny packs have pockets for two water bottles and a padded hip belt.

If you intend to do an extended, overnight trip, there are multiple considerations. First off, you need to decide what kind of framed pack you want. There are two backpack types for backpacking: the internal frame and the external frame. An internal frame pack rests closer to your body, making it more stable and easier to balance when hiking over rough terrain. An external frame pack is just that, an aluminum frame attached to the exterior of the pack. Some hikers consider an external frame pack to be better for long backpack trips because it distributes the pack weight better and allows you to carry heavier loads. It's often easier to pack, and your gear is more accessible. It also offers better back ventilation in hot weather.

The most critical measurement for fitting a pack is torso length. The pack needs to rest evenly on your hips without sagging. A good pack will come in two or three sizes and have straps and hip belts that are adjustable according to your body size and characteristics.

When you purchase a backpack, go to an outdoor store with salespeople who are knowledgeable in how to properly fit a pack. Once the pack is fitted for you, load the pack with the amount of weight you plan on taking on the trail. The weight of the pack should be distributed evenly and you should be able to swing your arms and walk briskly without feeling out of balance. Another good technique for evaluating a pack is to walk up and down stairs and make quick turns to the right and to the left to be sure the pack doesn't feel out of balance. Other features that are nice to have on a backpack include a removable day pack or fanny pack, external pockets for extra water, and extra lash points to attach a jacket or other items.

**Sleeping bags and pads.** Sleeping bags are rated by temperature. You can purchase a bag made with synthetic insulation, or you can buy a goose down bag. Goose down bags are more expensive, but they have a higher insulating capacity by weight and will keep their loft longer. You'll want to purchase a bag with a temperature rating that fits the time of year and conditions you are most likely to camp in. One caveat: The techno-standard for temperature ratings is far from perfect. Ratings vary from manufacturer to manufacturer, so to protect yourself you should purchase a bag rated 10° to 15° below the temperature you expect to be camping in. Synthetic bags are more resistant to water than down bags, but many down bags are now made with a Gore-Tex shell that helps to repel water. Down bags are also more compressible than synthetic bags and take up less room in your pack, which is an important consideration if you are planning a multiday backpack trip. Features to look for in a sleeping bag include a mummy style bag, a hood you can cinch down around your head in cold weather, and draft tubes along the zippers that help keep heat in and drafts out.

You'll also want a sleeping pad to provide insulation and padding from the cold ground. There are different types of sleeping pads available, from the more expensive self-inflating air mattresses to the less expensive closed-cell foam pads. Self-inflating air mattresses are usually heavier than closed-cell foam mattresses and are prone to punctures.

**Tents.** The tent is your home away from home while on the trail. It provides protection from wind, rain, snow, and insects. A three-season tent is a good choice for backpacking and can range in price from $100 to $500. These lightweight and versatile tents provide protection in all types of weather, except heavy snowstorms or high winds, and range in weight from four to eight pounds. Look for a tent that's easy to set up and will easily fit two people with gear. Dome type tents usually offer more headroom and places to store gear. Other handy tent features include a vestibule where you can store wet boots and backpacks. Some nice-to-have items in a tent include interior pockets to store small items and lashing points to hang a clothesline. Most three-season tents also come with stakes so you can secure the tent in high winds. Before you purchase a tent, set it up and take it down a few times to be sure it is easy to handle. Also, sit inside the tent and make sure it has enough room for you and your gear.

**Cell phones.** Many hikers are carrying their cell phones into the backcountry these days in case of emergency. That's fine and good, but please know that cell phone coverage is often poor to nonexistent in valleys, canyons, and thick forest. More importantly people have started to call for help because they're tired or lost. Let's go back to being prepared. You are responsible for yourself in the backcountry. Use your brain to avoid problems, and if you do encounter one, first use your brain to try to correct the situation. Only use your cell phone, if it works, in true emergencies. If it doesn't work down low in a valley, try hiking to a high point where you might get reception.

## Hiking with Children

Hiking with children isn't a matter of how many miles you can cover or how much elevation gain you make in a day; it's about seeing and experiencing nature through their eyes.

Kids like to explore and have fun. They like to stop and point out bugs and plants, look under rocks, jump in puddles, and throw sticks. If you're taking a toddler or young child on a hike, start with a trail that you're familiar with. Trails that have interesting things for kids, like piles of leaves to play in or a small stream to wade through during the summer, will make the hike much more enjoyable for them and will keep them from getting bored.

You can keep your child's attention if you have a strategy before starting on the trail. Using games is not only an effective way to keep a child's attention, it's also a great way to teach him or her about nature. Quiz children on the names of plants and animals. Pick up a family-friendly outdoor hobby like Geocaching (www.geocaching.com) or Letterboxing (www.atlasquest.com), both of which combine the outdoors, clue-solving, and treasure hunting. If your children are old enough, let them carry their own daypack filled with snacks and water. So that you are sure to go at their pace and not yours, let them lead the way. Playing follow the leader works particularly well when you have a group of children. Have each child take a turn at being the leader.

With children, a lot of clothing is key. The only thing predictable about weather is that it will change. Especially in mountainous areas, weather can change dramatically in a very short time. Always bring extra clothing for children, regardless of the season. In the winter, have your children wear wool socks and warm layers such as long underwear, a fleece jacket and hat, wool mittens, and good rain gear. It's not a bad idea to have these along in late fall and early spring as well. Good footwear is also important. A sturdy pair of high top tennis shoes or lightweight hiking boots are the best bet for little ones. If you're hiking in the summer near a lake or stream, bring along a pair of old sneakers that your child can put on when he wants to go exploring in the water. Remember when you're near any type of water, always watch your child at all times. Also, keep a close eye on teething toddlers who may decide a rock or leaf of poison oak is an interesting item to put in their mouth.

From spring through fall, you'll want your kids to wear a wide-brimmed hat to keep their face, head, and ears protected from the hot sun. Also, make sure your children wear sunscreen at all times. Choose a brand without PABA—children have sensitive skin and may have an allergic reaction to sunscreen that contains PABA. If you are hiking with a child younger than six months, don't use sunscreen or insect repellent. Instead, be sure that their head, face, neck, and ears are protected from the sun with a wide-brimmed hat, and that all other skin exposed to the sun is protected with the appropriate clothing.

Remember that food is fun. Kids like snacks so it's important to bring a lot of munchies for the trail. Stopping often for snack breaks is a fun way to keep the trail interesting. Raisins, apples, granola bars, crackers and cheese, cereal, and trail mix all make great snacks. Also, a few of their favorite candy treats can go a long way toward heading off a fit of fussing. If your child is old enough to carry her own backpack, let him or her fill it with some lightweight "comfort" items such as a doll, a small stuffed animal, or a little toy (you'll have to draw the line at bringing the ten-pound Tonka truck). If your kids don't like drinking water, you can bring some powdered drink mix or a juice box.

Avoid poorly designed child-carrying packs—you don't want to break your back carrying your child. Most child-carrying backpacks designed to hold a forty-pound child will contain a large carrying pocket to hold diapers and other items. Some have an optional rain/sun hood.

## Hiking with Your Dog

Bringing your furry friend with you is always more fun than leaving him behind. Our canine pals make great trail buddies because they never complain and always make good company. Hiking with your dog can be a rewarding experience, especially if you plan ahead.

**Getting your dog in shape.** Before you plan outdoor adventures with your dog, make sure he's in shape for the trail. Getting your dog into shape takes the same discipline as getting yourself into shape, but luckily, your dog can get in shape with you. Take your dog with you on your daily runs or walks. If there is a park near your house, hit a tennis ball or play Frisbee with your dog.

Swimming is also an excellent way to get your dog into shape. If there is a lake or river near where you live and your dog likes the water, have him retrieve a tennis ball or stick. Gradually build your dog's stamina up over a two- to three-month period. A good rule of thumb is to assume that your dog will travel twice as far as you will on the trail. If you plan on doing a 5-mile hike, be sure your dog is in shape for a 10-mile hike.

**Training your dog for the trail.** Before you go on your first hiking adventure with your dog, be sure he has a firm grasp on the basics of canine etiquette and behavior. Make sure he can sit, lie down, stay, and come. One of the most important commands you can teach your canine pal is to "come" under any situation. It's easy for your friend's nose to lead him astray or possibly get lost. Another helpful command is the "get behind" command. When you're on a hiking trail that's narrow, you can have your dog follow behind you when other trail users approach. Nothing is more bothersome than an enthusiastic dog that runs back and forth on the trail and disrupts the peace of the trail for others—or, worse, jumps up on other hikers and gets them muddy. When you see other trail users approaching you on the trail, give them the right of way by quietly stepping off the trail and making your dog lie down and stay until they pass.

**Equipment.** The most critical pieces of equipment you can invest in for your dog are proper identification and a sturdy leash. Flexi-leads work well for hiking because they give your dog more freedom to explore but still leave you in control. Make sure your dog has identification that includes your name and address and a number for your veterinarian. Other forms of identification for your dog include a tattoo or a microchip. You should consult your veterinarian for more information on these last two options.

The next piece of equipment you'll want to consider is a pack for your dog. By no means should you hold all of your dog's essentials in your pack—let him carry his own gear! Dogs that are in good shape can carry 30 to 40 percent of their own weight.

Most packs are fitted by a dog's weight and girth measurement. Companies that make dog packs generally include guidelines to help you pick out the size that's right for your dog. Some characteristics to look for when purchasing a pack for your dog include a harness that contains two padded girth straps, a padded chest strap, leash attachments, removable saddle bags, internal water bladders, and external gear cords.

You can introduce your dog to the pack by first placing the empty pack on his back and letting him wear it around the yard. Keep an eye on him during this first introduction. He may decide to chew through the straps if you aren't watching him closely. Once he learns to treat the pack as an object of fun and not a foreign enemy, fill the pack evenly on both sides with a few ounces of dog food in resealable plastic bags. Have your dog wear his pack on your daily walks for a period of two to three weeks. Each week add a little more weight to the pack until your dog will accept carrying the maximum amount of weight he can carry.

You can also purchase collapsible water and dog food bowls for your dog. These bowls are lightweight and can easily be stashed into your pack or your dog's. If you are hiking on rocky terrain or in the snow, you can purchase footwear for your dog that will protect his feet from cuts and bruises.

Always carry plastic bags to remove feces from the trail. It is a courtesy to other trail users and helps protect local wildlife.

The following is a list of items to bring when you take your dog hiking: collapsible water bowls, a comb, a collar and a leash, dog food, plastic bags for feces, a dog pack, flea/tick powder, paw protection, water, and a first-aid kit that contains eye ointment, tweezers, scissors, stretchy foot wrap, gauze, antibacterial wash, sterile cotton tip applicators, antibiotic ointment, and cotton wrap.

**First aid for your dog.** Your dog is just as prone—if not more prone—to getting in trouble on the trail as you are, so be prepared. Here's a rundown of the more likely misfortunes that might befall your canine friend.

*Bees and wasps.* If a bee or wasp stings your dog, remove the stinger with a pair of tweezers and place a mudpack or a cloth dipped in cold water over the affected area.

*Porcupines.* One good reason to keep your dog on a leash is to prevent it from getting a nose full of porcupine quills. You may be able to remove the quills with pliers, but a veterinarian is the best person to do this nasty job because most dogs need to be sedated.

*Heat stroke.* Avoid hiking with your dog in really hot weather. Dogs with heat stroke will pant excessively, lie down and refuse to get up, and become lethargic and disoriented. If your dog shows any of these signs on the trail, have him lie down in the shade. If you are near a stream, pour cool water over your dog's entire body to help bring his body temperature back to normal.

*Heartworm.* Dogs get heartworms from mosquitoes that carry the disease in the prime mosquito months of July and August. Giving your dog a monthly pill prescribed by your veterinarian easily prevents this condition.

*Plant pitfalls.* One of the biggest plant hazards for dogs on the trail are foxtails. Foxtails are pointed grass seed heads that bury themselves in your friend's fur, between his toes, and even get in his ear canal. If left unattended, these nasty seeds can work their way under the skin and cause abscesses and other problems. If you have a long-haired dog, consider trimming the hair between his toes and giving him a summer haircut to help prevent foxtails from attaching to his fur. After every hike, always look over your dog for these seeds—especially between his toes and his ears.

Other plant hazards include burrs, thorns, thistles, and poison oak. If you find any burrs or thistles on your dog, remove them as soon as possible before they become an unmanageable mat. Thorns can pierce a dog's foot and cause a great deal of pain. If you see that your dog is lame, stop and check his feet for thorns. Dogs are immune to poison oak but they can pick up the sticky, oily substance from the plant and transfer it to you.

*Protect those paws.* Be sure to keep your dog's nails trimmed so he avoids getting soft tissue or joint injuries. If your dog slows and refuses to go on, check to see that his paws aren't torn or worn. You can protect your dog's paws from trail hazards such as sharp gravel, foxtails, lava scree, and thorns by purchasing dog boots.

*Sunburn.* If your dog has light skin he is an easy target for sunburn on his nose and other exposed skin areas. You can apply a nontoxic sunscreen to exposed skin areas that will help protect him from overexposure to the sun.

*Ticks and fleas.* Ticks can easily give your dog Lyme disease, as well as other diseases. Before you hit the trail, treat your dog with a flea and tick spray or powder. You can also ask your veterinarian about a once-a-month pour-on treatment that repels fleas and ticks.

*Mosquitoes and deer flies.* These little flying machines can do a job on your dog's snout and ears. Best bet is to spray your dog with fly repellent for horses to discourage both pests.

*Giardia.* Dogs can get giardia, which results in diarrhea. It is usually not debilitating, but it's definitely messy. A vaccine against giardia is available.

*Mushrooms.* Make sure your dog doesn't sample mushrooms along the trail. They could be poisonous to him, but he doesn't know that.

When you are finally ready to hit the trail with your dog, keep in mind that national parks and many wilderness areas do not allow dogs on trails. Your best bet is to hike in national forests, BLM lands, and state parks. Always call ahead to see what the restrictions are.

# Hike Index

# About the Author

Andy Thompson first experienced the splendor of a Virginia waterfall in the mid-1990s when he leapt off a rock next to Panther Falls into the achingly cold Blue Ridge Mountain headwaters of the Pedlar River. Between that college rite of passage and today, Andy has crisscrossed the state by foot, boat, and two wheels in search of adventure. From 2007 to 2013 he was the Outdoors Columnist at the *Richmond Times-Dispatch*, where he covered everything from snakehead fishing in Northern Virginia to rabbit hunting in the Piedmont, from 100-mile mountain bike races near Harrisonburg (he didn't come in last) to hiking on the Appalachian Trail. Andy and his business partner now operate the outdoors-focused websites RichmondOutside.com and Terrain360.com. For the latter site, they created the first-ever 360-degree, surface-level image map of an entire river in the summer of 2014 when they floated the 348-mile James River in a custom pontoon raft, taking 360-degree pictures along the way.

Andy and his wife, Jess, live in Richmond, a burgeoning outdoors town, with their son, Sam, daughter, Ellie, and dogs Ruby and Lila. They live a stone's throw from the James, where bald eagles and osprey battle for turf, shad and striped bass run in the spring to spawn, and trails are filled with runners, bikers, birders, and every other stripe of outdoors lover.

*A view from the Blue Ridge Parkway is framed by the native Catawba rhododendron in full bloom.*

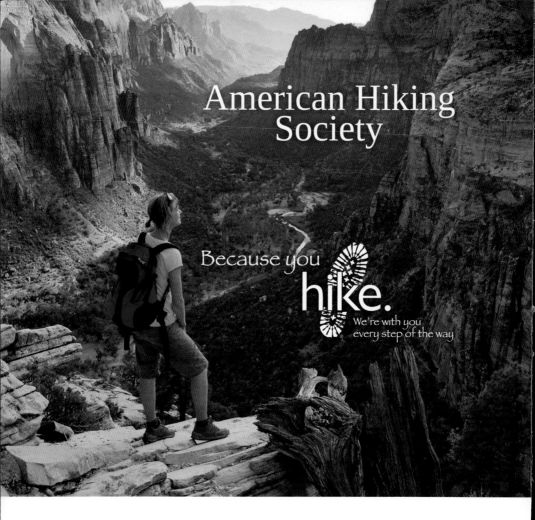

# American Hiking Society

Because you hike.

We're with you every step of the way

As a national voice for hikers, **American Hiking Society** works every day:

- Building and maintaining hiking trails
- Educating and supporting hikers by providing information and resources
- Supporting hiking and trail organizations nationwide
- Speaking for hikers in the halls of Congress and with federal land managers

Whether you're a casual hiker or a seasoned backpacker, become a member of American Hiking Society and join the national hiking community! You'll enjoy great member benefits and help preserve the nation's hiking trails, so tomorrow's hike is even better than today's. We invite you to join us now!

American Hiking Society

www.AmericanHiking.org • info@AmericanHiking.org